# Yoga and Meditation

**GEDDES &
GROSSET**

First published in this edition 2001 by Geddes & Grosset, an imprint of
Children's Leisure Products Limited

© 2001 Children's Leisure Products Limited, David Dale House,
New Lanark, ML11 9DJ, Scotland

Text first published 1999
Reprinted 1999, 2001

Cover image courtesy of PhotoDisc, Inc.

ISBN 1 84205 031 1

Printed and bound in the EU

# Contents

**Chapter 1 – Introduction** — 13
A stressful world — 13
Towards contentment — 14
What is meditation? — 15
What meditation is not: — 16
*Self-hypnosis* — 16
*Relaxation* — 17
*Necessarily tied to a religion* — 17
*Concentration* — 17
Stilling the mind — 17
Meditation and contemplation — 18
Yoga and meditation — 19
*What is yoga?* — 19
The first text — 23
The need for a teacher — 24
Keeping a level head — 26
Caveat! — 27
Crossing the bridge — 27

**Chapter 2 – Meditation in the World's Religions** — 29
Buddhism — 29
Zen Buddhism — 32
Christianity — 33
Hinduism — 36
Judaism — 37
Sufism — 39
Hare Krishna — 39

Taoism 41
 Yoga and religion 42
A note for nonbelievers 43

Chapter 3 – A Healthy Mind Equals
   a Healthy Body 45
Dualism 45
Mind and body 46
Stress 47
Meditation and stress 48
Meditation and smoking 49
Meditation and general wellbeing 50
Yoga and stress 51

Chapter 4 – How to Begin 53
Getting down to it 53
Posture 53
Easy posture 54
Siddhasana 54
Seven-point posture 55
Seven simple exercises 58
The sitting position 60
Kneeling (the Japanese posture) 60
Lying flat 61
Cupping the hands 62
Basic yoga exercises 62
  Before you begin 63
  The warm-up 64
  A beginner's regime 71

## Chapter 5 – The Meditation Session  83
Which technique?  84
Experiment  85
Proper breathing  85
The time . . .  86
. . . and the place  87
The meditation object  88
Problems  88
Physical tension  89
Long-term benefits  91
Breaking the spell  91

## Chapter 6 – Breathing Techniques  93
Awareness of breath  93
The simplest methods  94
Mindfulness of breathing meditation  95
Yoga breathing  97
*Pranayama*  98
*Holding the breath*  98
*The alternate nostril breath*  100
*The buzzing bee*  101
*The bellows breath*  101
*The cooling breath*  102
*The victorious breath (ujjayi)*  103
*The cleansing breath (kapalabhati)*  104
Control over responses  104
*Coping with anger and irritation*  105
*Coping with panic and anxiety*  106
*Taking in good or exciting news*  106

**Compartmentalisation**     **107**

**Chapter 7– Active Meditation**     **109**
**Collective meditation**     **109**
**The Sufi circle**     **110**
**Sensory awareness meditation**     **111**
**Tai Chi Ch'uan**     **112**
**Attention to life meditation**     **114**
**Meditation on the run**     **114**

**Chapter 8 – Mantras**     **117**
**Om**     **120**
**The Jesus prayer**     **120**
**The rosary**     **121**
**Humming like a bee**     **121**
**Transcendental meditation**     **122**
**Who says what:**     **123**
   *Buddhism*     *123*
   *Sikhism*     *124*
   *Hinduism*     *124*
   *Islam*     *124*
   *Judaism*     *125*
   *Christianity*     *125*
   *Sufism*     *126*

**Chapter 9– Visual Meditation**     **127**
**Tratek (gazing meditation)**     **127**
**Meditating on a candle**     **128**
**A flower or a bowl**     **129**

It takes practice     129
Many different symbols     130
Yantras and mandalas     131
Meditating with a mandala or yantra     133
The space between the eyebrows meditation     134
Colour visualising     134
Body of light visualising     135
Purification visualising     136
Bubbles of thought meditation     137
A visual stress buster     137
Visual meditation and health     138

**Chapter 10 – Advanced Meditation Techniques**     141
Inner heat meditation     141
Withdrawal of senses (pratyahara)     144
Concentration (dharana) and contemplation (dhyana)     146
*Practising dharana and dhyana*     148
*Visualisation*     150
*A visualisation journey*     151
Visualisation and the body     153
Nidra     154
The art of noise     155
Hamsa     156
Inner sounds (nadas)     156
Psychic powers     157
Self-realisation (samadhi)     158

**Chapter 11 – Other Techniques to Try**    **161**
**Tactile meditation**    **161**
**Music and meditation**    **161**
**Zen meditation**    **162**
  *Koan*    *163*

**Chapter 12 – Yoga: The Six Paths and**
   **the Eight Limbs**    **165**
**The six paths of yoga**    **165**
  *Bhakti yoga*    *165*
  *Gyana yoga*    *165*
  *Karma yoga*    *166*
  *Mantra yoga*    *166*
  *Hatha yoga*    *166*
  *Raja yoga*    *166*
**The eight limbs of yoga**    **167**
**The abstinences (yamas)**    **167**
  *Nonviolence (ahisma)*    *167*
  *Truthfulness (satya)*    *168*
  *Non-stealing (asteya)*    *168*
  *Continence (bramachanya)*    *168*
  *Non-possessiveness (aparigrapha)*    *169*
**The observances (niyamas)**    **169**
  *Purity (saucha)*    *169*
  *Contentment (santosha)*    *170*
  *Austerity (tapas)*    *171*
  *Study (svadhyaya)*    *172*
  *Attentiveness to the divine*
   *(ishvara pranidhana)*    *172*

**Chapter 13 – The Hatha Postures (Asanas)** 173
Diaphragm breathing 174
Mindfulness 176
Sitting, standing and lying positions 177
Beginning the session 178
The mountain (tadasana) 178
The cat 180
The cat (advanced) 181
The canoe 182
The triangle (trikonasana) 183
The tree (vrksasasana) 185
The cobra (bhujangasana) 186
The forward bend (paschimotanasana) 188
The bow (dhanurasana) 189
The bridge (satu bhandasana) 190
The wheel (chakrasana) (16) 192
The spinal twist (matsyendrasana) 193
The fish (matsyasana) (2) 195
The rabbit (3) 197
The dog (7) 199
The boat (4) 200
The peacock (mayurasana) 202
The fixed spot 203
The eagle (12) 204
The scissors (6) 205
The twist (10) 206
The leg lift (11) 208
The sideways leg lift (9) 210
The wide side-stretch (prasarita padottanasana) (19) 211

**The warrior (21)** 213
**The salute to the sun (surya namaskar)** 214
**Inverted postures** 223
  *The shoulder stand (sarvangasana) (8)* 223
  *The plough (halasana)* 225
  *The tripod* 226
  *The corpse posture (shavasana)* 228
**Advanced sitting positions** 229
  *The thunderbolt (vajrasana) (13)* 229
  *The cow-face* 230
  *The lion* 232
  *The Egyptian* 233
  *The tailor's position or easy posture* 234
  *The butterfly* 235
  *The half-lotus* 236
  *The lotus position (padmasana) (20)* 237
  *The fish-lotus* 238
**The importance of posture** 239
**The spine** 243

**Chapter 14 – The Chakras** 245
**Chakras** 245
**Maladhara** 248
**Swadisthana** 249
**Manipura** 249
**Anahata** 250
**Vissudha** 251
**Ajna** 251
**Sahasraha** 252

**Warning!** 252

**Kundalini** 253


**Chapter 15 – Ways to Unwind** 255

**Vipassana (the witnessing meditation)** 255

**Prarthana (the surrender meditation)** 256

**Zen driving** 256


**Chapter 16 – Grabbing the Moment Meditation** 259

**The wedding ring meditation** 259

**The red light meditation** 259

**Meditation at work** 260

**Spot meditation** 260

**Pain relief meditation** 260

**Countdown to calmness** 261

**Back to the future** 261


**Chapter 17 – Frequently Asked Questions** 263

**Is meditation selfish?** 263

**Can meditation help me sleep better?** 265


**Chapter 18 – Ten Reasons To Start Meditating** 267


**Chapter 19 – Two Case Studies** 271

**Mary** 271

**Shakyafinha** 273

**Postscript** 275


**A Glossary of Terms** 277

# Chapter 1

# Introduction

## A stressful world

In recent years, developments in science, technology and industry have accelerated. So have trends, and every season we are under pressure to dress in the latest style, to change our hairstyles, our eating habits, even where we put the furniture. Thousands of new book titles appear every year, challenging us to be well read and up to date, while dozens of TV channels and radio stations vie for our attention and subscription. Coupled with this is the fact that few of us have only a job to worry about, or children, or the household, or our health. Most of us are juggling several of these at one time, as well as trying to keep up with all the changes around us. Further, almost all of us struggle to be everything to all people: caring parent, fun-loving but sympathetic friend, dutiful child, and efficient employee.

While our minds reel with all these demands, our bodies develop tension headaches and muscular pains. We can't get to sleep at night, we drink and smoke too much, our relationships falter, our self-esteem plummets and our health suffers. Our world is undoubtedly a very stressful place, but learning to cope with stress is not the impossible task it may at first seem. What we have to learn is that our usual reactions to stress, such as drinking more heavily or pushing ourselves harder at work, are only making it worse. Physical exercise and relaxation go some way to redressing the balance, but our minds also require attention. After all, relaxed and happy people are healthier than stressed and miserable ones.

We have to learn how to take a step back, clear our heads, take a deep breath, and just be. If, for just a few minutes every day, everyone in the world did that, there would be considerably less heartache and strife.

## Towards contentment

In the words of the philosopher, Ludwig Wittgenstein, 'The world of those who are happy is different from the world of those who are not.' Meditation is the art of transcending our everyday thought processes and world view, if only for a very short period of time every other day. Our minds briefly escape the tyranny of worry and self-image, and we begin to get a sense of who we truly are and what we truly feel. If practised regularly, meditation will enhance our feelings of self-worth, and inevitably this will be reflected in the way we see the world. In short, by learning to like ourselves, we will also learn to like the world.

Meditation has physical benefits too. By enabling us to access inner calm, it helps us to alleviate stress, which is being linked to more and more physical ailments, from migraine to high blood pressure to heart and lung conditions. Meditation has also shown itself to be effective in the battle against addiction to alcohol and cigarettes.

Buddhism holds meditation at the heart of its practice, as do the other great oriental religions, such as Hinduism, whose most influential book, Bhagavad Gita, devotes an entire section to the practice of meditation and Sufism. In religious meditation, the sense of self-worth is linked to a feeling of being closer to God. Meditation also has its place in Western religions, such as Christianity and Judaism, but it does not require adherence to a particular faith to be successful.

Many people view meditation as peaceful but ineffectual self-centredness – in the words of one cynic, 'a form of self-indulgent, passive introversion'. They are wrong – the benefits to be gained from meditation in any of its various forms are many. Those who meditate regularly believe that it leads to a significant lowering of tension and negative emotions, while at the same time increasing efficiency at work and deepening the sense of inner calm.

This feeling of wellbeing brings physical benefits, for regular meditation eliminates or reduces stress, and who in the helter-skelter days of the beginning of the twenty-first century does not experience stress at some time or other? In reducing stress, meditation can ease migraine and tension headaches, reduce blood pressure, benefit the heart and reduce the discomfort of menstrual cramps.

## What is meditation?

In its simplest form, meditation is nothing more than allowing the mind to be lulled by a simple repetitive sensation – waves lapping on the beach, the tinkling of water from a fountain, repeating a word or sound over and over again, even something as mundane as the sound of machinery. Any of these, and countless others, can be used as something on which the mind focuses itself completely, thus putting worry and anxiety on the back-burner for a while. We have all done this naturally at some time or another: you may have gazed

15

into a beautiful sunset and become absorbed in the flames of colour, or been seduced by the lapping of waves on the sea-shore and the heat from the sun, or even simply closed your eyes and savoured the taste of a delicious meal. Children are much better at this than adults. Think of a child, bent over a half-finished painting, and think of the number of times he or she has to be called before they hear you telling them that their lunch is ready? The child is not ignoring you, he or she is simply too wrapped up in what they are doing to be dis-tracted by anyone or anything.

Put simply, meditation is me-time in its purest form: it is just being and letting the world around you just be as well. Used in a religious context, meditation is a means of com-muning directly with God, of focusing completely on him, and of seeing the world without the blinkers of selfish, worldly thought.

Meditation need not be a time-consuming process (twenty minutes a day are all that is needed). Practised properly, it is a voyage during which preconceived notions and ideas fade, the senses and the intellect are refined, and the ability to concentrate is increased.

Its benefits quickly become apparent, and those who prac-tise it often say that the day they first took to meditation on a regular basis was a watershed in their lives.

## What meditation is not:
### Self-hypnosis
Which requires the participant to reach a state of semicon-scious trance. Meditation is very much about the 'here and now' and its aim is to enable the meditator to 'live in the moment'.

*Relaxation*
Which is essentially passive, whereas meditation is an active focusing of the mind. While meditation attempts to transcend the normal thought processes, relaxation will often engage those very patterns of thought. However, meditation can be a great aid to relaxation, and relaxation a great aid to meditation.

*Necessarily tied to a religion*
Although meditation is used in all world religions, it does not specifically belong to any one nor is there any need for it to be tied to religion at all. Meditation can prove just as positive and spiritual an experience for an atheist as for a Buddhist.

*Concentration*
Which can be a means of achieving transcendence, but is not the object of the exercise. Concentrating on one thing is only a means to clearing the mind of all other thoughts. The object of your concentration is not important in itself, and, in fact, many meditators choose deliberately meaningless words or objects on which to concentrate for this very reason.

**Stilling the mind**
All day, every day, our minds are whirling to the tune of their own 'internal drama'. Not only are we subject to constant sensory input, from the rumble of traffic to that of our stomachs, but our reaction to every single incident, every scrap of memory, every concern about the future, be it tomorrow, next week, or after we die, are all tumbling through

our minds like a noisy machine-load of multicoloured washing. Often, after a hectic day at work, or a row with a partner or friend, it is very difficult to switch off.

Who hasn't, at one time or another, wasted an entire evening ranting about someone at work who has annoyed them? And who has never been told, when extremely upset or angry, that we 'aren't ourselves'? Because, when this internal shouting match is never still, we are never at peace, and who we really are is completely overwhelmed by our emotions. We become the sum total of our thoughts, rather than the instigator and controller of them.

To stop this, the mind must be stilled, all thoughts put on hold. To rediscover that our thoughts are under our control is incredibly liberating and empowering. We must realise that we do not have to fail at giving up smoking just because we have all the previous times and a little voice is telling us that we are weak-willed and won't be able to cope. You do not have to avoid doing certain things just because your mind runs through its catalogue of fears every time you try to break the cycle.

Taking control enables you to see things as they really are, without being hindered by associative thoughts. Taking control allows us to respond more appropriately, because our response is direct, based on the here and now. Regular meditation helps you to live in the here and now, and to see yourself as the controller of your own mind and thoughts. In so doing, it also helps you to truly experience what happens to you.

## Meditation and contemplation

Confusion sometimes arises when the words 'meditation' and 'contemplation' are used interchangeably. A working distinction between the two is that meditation can be considered a preparatory step and contributory to the achievement of contemplation.

Meditation involves concentration, narrowing the focus of attention to a single theme, catechism or doctrine while remaining cognitive and intellectual. Contemplation is a direct intuitive seeing, using spiritual facilities that are beyond discursive thought. In the words of Richard of Saint-Victor, a twelfth-century theologian, 'Meditation investigates, contemplation wonders.'

## Yoga and meditation
### What is yoga?
Stop what you are doing. Stand up, take a deep breath and have a really good stretch. Standing on tiptoes, make yourself as tall as possible with your hands reaching up to the sky and your fingers splayed. Breathe out slowly, and slowly resume your normal standing posture. Now doesn't that feel good? Can you feel the blood tingling in your hands and feet? Do the muscles in your arms and legs feel relaxed and yet energised? Does your mind, be it only for a fleeting moment, seem to have taken a breather from its daily round of thoughts and worries? If your answer is yes, then you are feeling the benefits of yoga already.

Yoga is a system of physical and mental exercises designed to instil a sense of tranquillity and wellbeing in the practitioner. Its origins are lost in the mists of time, though estimates suggest that it has been practised in India for over five thousand years, and is believed to have been inspired by the contemplation of animals, particularly cats, as they stretched. Observers noted that, after a good stretch and arch, the animal's energy and altertness was increased, and so they sought to utilise this knowledge for human benefit. To this day, many yoga positions are named after the creatures they were adapted from: the tortoise, the cobra, the butterfly.

Yoga is a technique of self-awareness that integrates the mind and the body. By uniting the two, yoga helps to control negative and destructive thought patterns and assist the mind to work with, rather than against, the body. Hatha yoga teaches techniques of physical control of the body through postures known as asanas (*see* Chapter 13) and breathing techniques called pranayama. The asanas make the body supple and benefit the neuromuscular system, each posture combining mental acuity with breathing techniques and a specific body movement. Pranayama builds up the body's energy.

Regular practice of the asanas and breathing exercises will induce a more positive frame of mind, not just during the exercises but throughout daily life. You will find that you are less prone to mood swings, and that you feel less at the mercy of external forces as you have developed an increased degree of inner strength.

Knowing yourself the yoga way is quite a different thing from knowing your habits, likes and dislikes. In fact, having fixed ideas about yourself can often obscure your true nature, as you shut yourself off from experiences, or tell yourself, in advance, how you are going to react. For instance, if you believe that you are an impatient person who needs fast results, then you will become frustrated by the slow results of yoga, and perhaps give up without giving yourself a chance. If, instead, you try turning this assumption about yourself on its head, and tell yourself that actually you have infinite reserves of patience, you will surprise yourself by having just such reserves. Bear this in mind when you practise your asanas too. If you believe that you are stiff and unsupple, the exercises will be tough. If, instead, you convince yourself that there is a super-supple person inside you just itching to get out, you will begin to feel a real difference. It is important to approach yoga with an open mind, and to shed feelings of pride and desire. This is called 'transcending the ego'. Far from being the self-abnegation that it sounds, transcending your ego is actually extremely liberating.

If you are still resistant to the idea of finding your true self, perhaps because you feel that you are already very well acquainted, thank you very much, then consider how many times in your life you have felt that you are acting 'out of character'. An occasion perhaps when you drank more alcohol than usual, said things you didn't mean, or had unaccountable mood swings. We do this when we are unhappy and out of touch with ourselves, usually due to stress and being constantly bombarded by external pressures that give us no time or freedom to look into ourselves. Certainly there are few people who can claim that they never behave differently with different people and in different environments, sometimes endorsing opinions that they do not believe in, and acting against their instincts. Occasions like this often leave us feeling unworthy, and lacking in integrity. The impulse to behave this way generally arises from a lack of self-confidence and a lack of a sense of our own selves.

Now consider how it feels to be happily in love. This is not to be confused with the intense infatuation characterised by highs and lows, but the later, more relaxed stage. When in love, we feel as if we have found our destiny and that everything in the world is in its right place. We feel slightly removed from ordinary life, and less thrown by external events. We feel that we can cope with everything, from big red electricity bills to three weeks of flu. In fact, being in love makes us more immune to disease, and makes our skin clearer and our eyes sparkling. Yet, for all that we are removed, we feel as if our senses have been fine tuned, making us alert to sounds and colours, so that we feel we are really seeing the world around us. We feel alive and at the centre of our being. Discovering your true self produces similar feelings of awareness and oneness.

Some people feel afraid of uncovering their true selves, regarding it as a sort of frightening therapy process wherein they will be forced to confront aspects of their nature with which they are uncomfortable. This is not so. Raja yoga, which focuses on the mental aspects, is not a form of therapy in the psychoanalytic sense. Rather it is tapping into the essence of your being, the spirit from which you sprang. Indeed, this realisation of the inner self can provide enormous support when dealing with difficult personal problems, and a way of giving yourself temporary release from them.

Even if we are free of deep troubles and have sufficient confidence to be ourselves, we all live in a very manic, busy world, which bombards us with multifarious messages about how we should live and what we should think. Women especially tend to feel that they are pulled this way and that by contradictory demands, to be feminine but independent, good mothers but also good workers, and so on. Sometimes we need a touchstone, a talisman for instance, a place, or even a person, towards which we can reach when we feel the need to 'touch base' and work things out. In ancient communities there would be wise woman or man who could counsel those who felt out of sorts and confused. Our equivalent today, perhaps, is the agony aunt! When we achieve self-knowledge we become our own touchstone, the person we can rely on.

Yoga is a means of seeing things as they really are rather than as they seem. In yoga, all body and mental tensions have to cease if this end is to be achieved. Accordingly, one of the basic yoga techniques is meditation, which turns our consciousness towards the inner calm helping us to achieve samadhi, or pure consciousness.

## The first text

The first written yoga system is the *Yoga Sutras of Pantajali*, dating from around 200 to 400 BC. Written in the ancient language of Sanskrit, Pantajali's text is the earliest collation and systematisation of an ancient knowledge that was previously handed down in the oral tradition. The *Yoga Sutras* are not advised as a teach-yourself companion, as they are extremely complex, but rather as a guide for teachers to adapt.

According to Pantajali, yoga brings about the suspension of the mind's waves (vrittis), resulting in mindfulness, which means the ability to pay attention to your life. To put it in modern terminology, to 'wake up and smell the coffee' or 'get real'. This means experiencing what is happening around and within you, rather than being consumed by internal mental convolutions while life passes you by – thus avoiding the situation as described by W. H. Auden: 'In headaches and in worry/Vaguely life leaks away.'

To achieve these, Pantajali advocates practice (abhaysa) and non-attachment (vairagya). The latter does not necessitate the abandonment of all worldly goods, but a relinquishment of assumptions about yourself and the world. Consider how many times you duck opportunities because you are 'not right for it', either because you feel you are not capable of it, or because it is not suited to you. Many modern psychologists would tell us, in no uncertain terms, that we are wrong in these self-judgements, and that in fact we do not really know ourselves at all. Our beliefs are often based upon a hotchpotch of experience (often misleading), upon other people's opinions, and our fears and prejudices. If this seems absurd, consider the reaction of children to new experiences: curious, eager and positive, they embrace the unknown, unhindered by accumulated memories and assumptions. Experience, in a sense, actually blinkers us to the world, and hobbles our development.

## The need for a teacher

No one in their right mind would sit down at a piano and expect to play a Chopin nocturne if they had never played before. So why should someone who is about to meditate for the first time sit down and expect to lose themselves in meditation right away? Like all things worth doing, the best way to learn meditation and yoga is to study with someone who has already mastered it. If we are to compare the mind with a piano, in order to create beautiful music, we need to study with an expert who is familiar with the instrument and who can assist us to gain mastery over it.

A good teacher must be qualified, compassionate, expert, patient, sincere and sympathetic, and someone in whom the pupil has complete confidence. But where do you find such a paragon? Whether you are religious or not, a good person to guide you in the ways of meditation is an established religious teacher, such as a rabbi or a priest. It is highly unlikely that he or she would discourage a nonbeliever's quest for inner peace, and religious groups are rarely averse to the idea of nonbelievers sitting in with them during silent worship. Further, there are a great number of religious books, from all faiths, that teach the art of meditation.

Apart from religious teachers, there are qualified therapists who, if they cannot teach you themselves, could certainly point you in the direction of someone who could.

Some novices are lucky and find the right 'guru' straight away. Others may take months, even years before they meet the one who is right for them. Those who fall into the latter category should not be disheartened. They should carry on practising basic meditation techniques, trying different teachers and following their own judgement until, eventually, they find someone who can help them to get the most out of meditation.

Like a therapist or a doctor, your teacher should be someone you feel you can trust. Many people also find it important that their teacher is a good role model. After all, who will feel confident learning techniques to enhance inner calm from a person who is visibly stressed, abuses drugs and alcohol, drives like a maniac, or has affairs with his or her 'students'?

Do not be persuaded to part with large sums of cash by promises of masterly teaching. No one can predict exactly what technique will suit you, and no method is superior to another. The ideal teacher for you, just like the ideal technique, will only be found by a process of patient trial and error. Bear in mind, however, that even the greatest teacher can do nothing for you unless, like a pianist, you are willing to put in the practice.

Some people will prefer not to have a teacher at all, or be unable to find someone suitable. Instead they might take their instruction from books, lectures, courses and retreats. There are also many audio and visual tapes on the market, aimed at the increasing numbers of people who are turning to meditation either for health or spiritual reasons. Before committing yourself to the expense of buying one, inquire at your local library to find out if it has an audio section. If there is such a tape on its shelves, borrow it for a few days to find out if it helps you.

## Keeping a level head

Where you meditate and when you meditate is up to you, but a word of advice – don't be tempted to adopt a holier-than-thou attitude among friends and colleagues. You must remember that one of the most important lessons in meditation is that the subjugation of the ego is necessary if you are to transcend your normal state of mind. Rivalry with other meditators is also counterproductive. And what could be more ridiculous than two people arguing about who is the most at peace?

Friends may, after some weeks or months, realise that you appear to be calmer and more relaxed and that you have changed subtly in some way that they cannot put their finger on. They may ask you what has brought about the change. Then by all means tell them that you have taken up meditating but broadcasting your experiences can defeat the object of the exercise!

## Caveat!

When you begin practising meditation you may experience a 'honeymoon' period, when you feel much more positive and relaxed. However, this may not last. Meditation is about being your real self and, therefore, aspects of yourself which you may not like will eventually bubble to the surface, providing a less than blissful focus for your thoughts. At this point, many drift away from meditation, feeling discouraged by this 'pain barrier'. However, if you persevere, that initial bliss will return.

A word of warning though. Most people can cope with the bad things in themselves, but some people cannot. An obsessive personality may find themselves locked into focusing on a part of themselves they cannot cope with, and this could be extremely dangerous.

Anyone who is suffering from clinical depression or any mild form of mental illness should first consult his or her doctor.

Meditation should never be used as a substitute for medical treatment, and anyone on any form of medication should likewise consult his or her doctor.

Meditation creates an altered state of consciousness. Newcomers have no way of knowing how they will respond to it, so it is best to limit the first few sessions to ten minutes at most.

Finally, meditation should not be seen as a panacea. It should be seen as a means to an end, not as the end in itself.

## Crossing the bridge

In his book *Complete Meditation*, American guru Steve Kravette wrote, 'By practising meditation and being completely who you are, you will become more than you are now. You will be able to cross the next evolutionary bridge and begin to develop the full potential of your creaturehood.' Meditation is a journey, enjoy it.

# Chapter 2

## Meditation in the World's Religions

### Buddhism

Meditation lies at the very centre of Buddhism, the term used in the West to describe the teachings of an Indian prince, Guatama Siddhartha, who lived from *c*.563 BC to 483 BC. Siddhartha's wealthy father did everything he could to protect his son from the evils of the world and it was not until the young man was in his late twenties that he saw a beggar, a sick man, a decrepit old man and a corpse for the first time and realise d just how privileged he was. When he asked a wandering monk about sickness and suffering, the mendicant told him that misery and pain were part and parcel of everyday life. Inspired by the monk's example, Siddhartha left his wife and family and turned his back on wealth and self-indulgence.

At first he looked to Hinduism for answers to the problems of suffering but, finding no answers in the faith of his ancestors, he began to conduct his own search for the truth and meaning of life.

Six years later, sitting deep in thought in the shade of a bo tree on the banks of the River Neranjari he achieved enlightenment and, seeing it as his duty to help others along the path he had trodden for so long, he began to preach his message.

In Buddhism it is important that, having achieved enlightenment, one then returns with it 'to the marketplace', that is, teaches it for the benefit of other people. The Buddha taught that insight would be achieved not through self-indulgence (which hinders spiritual growth) nor self-denying fanaticism (which is physically and mentally dangerous), but by following The Middle Way.

Like other Indian religions, Buddhism subscribes to the idea of karma, which is the belief that we experience the consequences of all our actions and thoughts. Because Buddhism also subscribes to the concept of reincarnation, these consequences may be felt in the next life, or the one after this. Thus are we trapped in a cycle of birth and death, which can only be transcended and escaped by following The Middle Way. This latter demands trust (until they can see for themselves) in the Four Noble Truths, which are:

- All life is suffering
- Suffering is caused by ignorance of what we are, which leads us to desire transitory pleasures that cannot make us happy
- Suffering will end when we realise what we are and stop desiring transitory pleasures
- To find out who we are, we must follow The Middle Way.

It also requires those who seek enlightenment to have the right values, the right speech, conduct themselves in the right manner and have the right means of livelihood. They must endeavour in the right way, have right control of their minds and have the right kind of meditation.

One of the major disciplines of the Buddhist meditator is to attain 'unification of the mind' by eliminating all distractions. As the practitioner learns to meditate for long periods, agitation, scepticism and doubt disappear and are replaced by a feeling of bliss. The meditator becomes absorbed in thought (a process known as jhana) and moves deeper and deeper until he or she finally acquires an awareness of infinite space.

Many Buddhists regard the pursuit of various jhana levels as secondary to the 'Path of Mindfulness', which in the end leads to nirvana. The meditator learns to break out of stereotyped thought and comes to perceive every moment of everyday reality as if it were a new event. The ego shrinks in importance; the universe is seen to be in a state of total and ever-changing flux. This realisation leads to a sense of detachment from the world of experience, an abandonment of all desires, the abolition of self-interest and, ultimately, the ego itself.

Meditation can take place anywhere, for Buddhism is essentially a religion for the individual. Meditation is not a communal act. Even within organised Buddhist communities, the way one meditates is a matter for the individual and not for the community. There is no prescribed pattern of worship for Buddhists. They may, if they so wish, visit pagodas, temples and shrines and focus on something there while they are meditating. However, it is equally proper for them to meditate in their own homes, sitting in whichever position they choose (usually cross-legged) on the floor.

Some Buddhist families may have a statue of the Buddha in a specially built shrine in their homes; some burn incense and use prayer beads to help them concentrate the mind; some use mantras (*see* page 117) and mandalas (*see* page 131), while others simply adopt their usual meditative position and quickly lose themselves in meditation.

It is estimated that more than 300 million people around the world practise Buddhism, and it is an interesting comment on late twentieth-century life that more and more young people in the West are treading the same path and that Buddhism is one of the fastest-growing religions in the Western world.

## Zen Buddhism

According to legend, in AD 520 the Indian thinker Bodhidharma (the first patriarch of Zen Buddhism) journeyed from India to China, where he presented himself at the court of the Emperor Wu, a devout Buddhist. When the emperor asked Bodhidharma what merit he, the emperor, had gained on the Path to Enlightenment by building temples and assiduously copying holy writings, the Indian incurred his wrath by telling him that there was no merit in such deeds as they showed worldly attachment. True merit was only to be found in acts of absolute wisdom, beyond the realm of rational thought. 'Truth,' he said, 'is emptiness, and holiness for holiness' sake has nothing to recommend it.'

Wu was so furious with Bodhidharma's doctrine that the Indian left court and spent several years in a monastery contemplating a wall. He later communicated his thoughts and teachings – the Visudd-himagga, or Path to Purification, which describes the meditative approach from the Buddhist point of view – to Hui-k'o who thus became the second patriarch of Zen Buddhism.

Meditation has always been a keystone of Buddhism. Zen teaches that it is everything. Through meditation a Zen Buddhist will realise his or her true self, that is, find the Buddha that lives within us all. To achieve this, all inner conflicts must be resolved. This stilling of the mind reaps psychological, physical and spiritual dividends. Apart from being generally more serene than others, Zen Buddhists also tend to have a very positive approach to their health, listening to their bodies without waiting for the spur of physical crisis. Its followers do not believe in rituals or reading the Buddha's sermons (sutras). In Zen, meditation is more total and more intense than in any other Buddhist sect. The Buddhist who follows the Zen path must strive to avoid all conscious thought except the point on which he or she is meditating (*see* Zen meditation page 162).

There is a famous story of a man who went to a Zen master and asked to be taught Zen. The master said nothing but poured the seeker a cup of tea, using a cup that was already full, and kept pouring until the pot was empty. Then he spoke.

'You are like this cup,' he said. 'You are full. How can I pour Zen into you? Empty yourself and come back.'

Zen has two schools: Rinzai and Soto. Rinzai uses koans, or unanswerable questions – such as 'What is the sound of one hand clapping?' or 'Where was your face before you were born?' – to help the mind break free from the confines of logical thought. Soto Zen perfects the art of sitting and doing nothing, in order to focus the mind on the present moment. Both have the same goal: to see reality as it is, rather than as we are conditioned to see it. Satori is the name given to the experience of truly seeing reality.

## Christianity

Modern Christianity stresses the importance of doing good deeds, loving one's neighbour and avoiding sin; the mystical side of the religion has largely been swept aside. But

Christianity is essentially a mystical religion, for the true Christian seeks to be united with God through following the way of Christ, who said, 'I am the way, the truth and the light. No one comes to the Father except through me.'

Meditation should play an important part in Christian worship, and it is interesting to note in this respect the volume of music that has been composed down the centuries to encourage meditation. The Gregorian chants and plainsong of the early centuries were intended to focus the worshippers' thoughts on God. This mesmerising music is still very popular today, and taped versions of it are used as a soothing background for such therapies as acupressure and aromatherapy, and as an aid to meditation. The solemn, silent atmosphere of a church is also conducive to meditative thought. For instance, visitors to the basilica of the Sacre Coeur at Montmartre in Paris, no matter how noisy they were at the portals, are invariably reduced to respectful silence once they enter the very awe-inspiring and sacred atmosphere. Many find that their thoughts turn to more spiritual matters than the next tourist attraction, and line up to light candles and close their eyes in a short prayer.

Traditional Christian teaching advocates meditation as a means of getting closer to God. St Teresa of Avila, for example, recommended the *via positiva* – concentrating the mind on God's love and absolute goodness in order to acquire some sense of His magnitude. St Teresa began the tradition of silent meditation and contemplative prayer that is the mainstay of the Carmelite orders. Carmelite nuns receive countless daily requests for prayers, and their raison d'etre is to answer these requests, as well as pray for those who cannot or have not asked them, such as those of another faith or nationality, or those in too much trouble.

It is through such contemplation that the Christian meditator strives to overcome the limitations of conscious thought and achieve a state of ecstasy in the perfect union with God in love and adoration.

St Teresa of Avila's message was that if you surrender to God's work, and give up all your preconceived ideas of who and what He is, you will be able to commune with Him properly. This is akin to the non-religious idea of surrendering old ideas and thoughts in order to properly commune with the self, and therefore the world. This surrendering of the will is also prescribed for times of deep psychological distress, such as is felt when one fears the loss of faith or that prayer has ceased to have any meaning.

Meditation is still widely practised in monasteries, convents and other religious communities, and more and more Christians are spending time 'in retreat', sometimes for a day or two, sometimes for longer, in quiet contemplation.

Christian meditation usually concentrates on the life of Jesus, Mary and the saints, and the most common aid to meditation is probably the Crucifix, although some Christians find that their concentration is heightened if they repeat the name of Jesus or Mary, or recite short prayers while they meditate (see pages 120–121).

St Ignatius Loyola, the founder of the Jesuits, used a type of internal visualisation of the life of Christ for a course of meditation. His Spiritual Exercises were initially used in the training of Jesuits, but have been used over the centuries by many Christians who wish to meditate and develop their spiritual life.

In the Eastern Orthodox Church, icons are still used as a focus for meditation. These religious icons are prepared with utmost care and ceremony. The wood and paint are blessed and the painter of the icon adheres to strict religious observances and executes the icon in a meditative state. It is important to remember that the icon itself is not the object of worship but the focus, in much the same way as a Tibetan mandala (*see* pages 131–133).

Quakers gather for silent worship, meditating together on a particular theme, often that of other people or nations in crisis. Many experience a sense of being 'connected' with the other worshippers, and feel that their meditations are the stronger for this connectedness.

## Hinduism

There is no formal creed in Hinduism, rather a number of religious concepts have developed and have been elaborated since it was founded, probably about 3000 years ago. These ideas were centred on the aim of every Hindu, which is to attain ultimate freedom, or moksha, to be free of the endless cycle of rebirths and to be at one with Brahman – the one ultimate reality. Humans learn through yoga (the word derives from the Sanskrit yuj, meaning 'to bind together') to achieve this union.

It is probably with yoga that most Westerners associate meditation. A few years ago the mention of the word would conjure up images of scraggy men, dressed in loincloths, sitting in a meditative trance, Indeed, stories were circulated of yogis who had been in such a state for so long that birds had nested on their heads. Westerners who 'did yoga' were regarded at best as cranks, but today, with more and more people in the West taking it up and with a new interest in oriental religion generally, if someone confesses to trying yoga, the reaction is generally one of interest and an expressed desire to know more.

The rise of interest in yoga meditation probably came in the 1960s with the huge publicity given to the pop groups who travelled to India and returned extolling the virtues of transcendental meditation. Unfortunately, and perhaps the reason why transcendental meditation is still often regarded with suspicion, it tended, in the public consciousness, to be identified with other, so called, hippy pursuits, such as reckless drug-taking and promiscuity.

But what was new to the West has been practised for thousands of years in the subcontinent. Yoga, the means of gaining liberation from the senses, is one of the four main concepts that underpin Hindu spiritual philosophy. The others are karma, the law of causality that links mankind to the universe, maya, the illusion of the manifest world, and nirvana, the absolute reality that lies beyond illusion. The concept of yoga in Hinduism and in other religions is discussed later in this chapter.

## Judaism

'When a man strips away the material aspect which envelops him, he will depict in his mind only the divine energy, so that its light will be of infinite greatness.' The words of Rabbi Dov Baer underline the importance of meditation in Jewish mysticism, which has its roots in the Kaballa, the ancient tradition that combines a complex system of philosophy with specific techniques for increasing spiritual awareness.

Kaballistic teaching holds that everything in the universe is derived from one source and that the purpose of our existence is to recognise our identity with God and all of creation through meditation and other spiritual practises.

Hassidic Jews took the teachings of the Kaballa and spread them to the people (rather than leaving them to the mystic few), just as the Buddha did when he achieved enlightenment. Meditative prayers are considered to be at their most effective when made for the sake of God, not the person praying. If a worshipper can forget his needs and lose himself in his praise 'it may then happen that his request will be granted because it resulted in his turning to God in prayer', according to Rabbi Judah Laib Alter, a Hassidic master.

A nonbeliever might suggest that the worshipper got what he wanted because he was in touch with his own being and therefore would only have asked for something he truly wanted, that is, not transitory or worldly riches.

Kaballistic Jews most often practise visual meditation (*see* page 127), focusing their thoughts on the Tree of Life or the characters of the Jewish alphabet, each of which is said to contain an aspect of the creative energy. They believe that by focusing the mind on various combinations of divine names and characters a divine energy is released which not only spiritually enriches them, but also the world itself.

Jews who follow the meditative path claim that they are open to a state of awareness that transcends their normal level of consciousness. They hold that their physical health also benefits. This is in line with the teaching of early Jewish mystics, who recognise d the relationship between a person's state of mind and his or her physical wellbeing.

## Sufism

Some say that Sufism (the word comes from 'sufi' and was originally applied to someone who wore suf, or undyed wool) developed from Islam. Others believe that it developed as a reaction against it. Whatever its origins, most Sufis are Muslim, although the latter is not a prerequisite of the former, and non-Islamic Sufi groups are found in many parts of the world.

Sufis base their beliefs on certain passages of the Koran, and some early Christian ideas. Their aim is to transcend everyday thought processes and to achieve a mystical union of the physical, the spiritual and the mental. The Sufist way of life involves fasting, storytelling, dancing and meditation.

There are many different types of meditation and many daily activities are ascribed a particular significance which, in effect, makes them meditations. Perhaps the most unusual is one practised by a particular group of Sufists – the Mevlevi, or whirling dervishes – who achieve a state of meditative ecstasy by spinning round and round at an ever-increasing rate, hoping to empty the mind of everything apart from communicating with God. It is a highly complex form of meditation in which all the dancers are in unity while, simultaneously, each uniquely experiences the ecstasy of divine communion. Most forms of meditation can be performed easily in the home, whirling, however, should not.

## Hare Krishna

Born in America in 1966 of his Divine Grace A C Bhatstivedanta Swami Prabhupada, but with its roots in ancient religions, Hare Krishna was embraced by the so-called hippy movement. Unfortunately, this lead to various false public perceptions about the religion which its devotees are, today, still struggling to overcome.

Hare Krishna devotees are non-drinking, non-gambling, non-promiscuous vegetarians, who believe themselves, and indeed all of mankind, to be part of the supreme consciousness that is Krishna. Their well-ordered days begin early with chanting rounds of Japa (the holy names of God). This chanting, like the Sufist practice of whirling, is deployed because it is often difficult to clear the mind sufficiently to meditate. Their chant, the Maha Mantra, is composed of Sanskrit names for God, and as Krishna is non-different from his name, Hare Krishna devotees believe that they are actually associating with the higher consciousness when they use his name. Through chanting they are also clearing their minds of all conditioning and worldly illusions, and thus discovering their real selves behind the roles that they play in everyday life.

According to the *Upanishads* (the sacred Sanskrit books outlining the mystic doctrines of ancient Hindu philosophy), 'Life comes from the spirit itself. Even as a man casts a shadow, so the spirit itself casts the shadow of life.' In the same spirit, Hare Krishnas believe that only by embracing one's spirituality, i.e., the source of life, can one truly experience existence. Hare Krishna meditation, being the method by which to embrace one's spirituality, is the key to appreciating existence.

In her biography *I, Tina*, written with Kurt Loder, Tina Turner describes how daily chanting enabled her, first of all, to cope with the difficulties of her domestic situation, and then, to find the inner strength to do something about it. Chanting, she discovered, enabled her to shut out the voices of people telling her what to do and how to feel, and listen to her own inner voice. It is not therefore only a tool for religious devotion, but also a valuable aid to self-discovery.

Hare Krishnas are very open to nonbelievers and centres offer free (vegetarian) meals and classes on meditation, as well as the Hare Krishna faith, without any obligation to join them.

## Taoism

Founded in the sixth century by Lao-Tzu, author of the *Tao Te Ching*, Taoism concerns itself with the underlying reality that pervades all of existence – the Tao, which cannot be described in words. According to Taosim, everything has a counterpart: dark and light, good and evil, man and woman. Like Yin and Yang (the complementary principles of Chinese philosophy), these things are not opposed, but part of a whole.

It is pointless trying to oppose this natural order of things, including progress, but that does not mean that Taoism is passive. Rather, it is about fitting in with, adapting to, the flow, just as a fish adapts itself to the varying currents of a stream.

Taoist meditation, or 'non-doing' as it is referred to, is a focusing of the mind and body on the Tao. By doing so, the meditator hopes to realign himself to changes in the flow, and virtue and wellbeing will arise naturally once he is re-attuned.

**NB:** The modern, religious, interpretation of Taoism, concerned largely with magic and eternal life, is quite different from the philosophy mentioned above. In fact, eternal life is a concept that Lao-Tzu would have abhorred, as death is the necessary counterbalance to life, and so gives the latter its significance.

## Yoga and religion

The *Upanishads*, the ancient sacred books outlining the mystical and esoteric doctrines of Hindu philosophy, and dating from around 500 BC, make much reference to yoga. The initial effects of practice are described as a feeling of 'lightness' and a clearer complexion – two greatly desired states in the modern world. However, the ultimate goal is to achieve samadhi, a higher consciousness that is characterised by a feeling of oneness with the universe. Ego is transcended and the individual self (atman) becomes one with the universal self (brahman).

The *Bhagavad Gita*, perhaps the most famous text, dating from 300 to 400 BC, describes yoga as the means to achieving enlightenment, in the context of the Hindu tradition of spiritual discipline. However, Hinduism is by no means intrinsic to yoga. All world religions seek to reintegrate the worshipper with the supreme being, and yoga practitioners of all denominations report an increased sense of their own spirituality thanks to the disciplines of yoga. It is all too easy to worship by rote, saying the prayers, reading the texts, observing the duties, without experiencing the joy of faith and a feeling of union with the creator. Yoga enables many to do this.

Of course, yoga does not require religious belief at all, which is one of the reasons why it will be around for a long, long time to come. More and more people are turning away from orthodox religion, and instead are seeking to discover a personal sense of spirituality – their own bespoke religion, if you like, based on personally felt tenets of belief. Yoga is an excellent means of tapping into this.

Even if spirituality is not something that interests you, yoga is also beneficial in enhancing your enjoyment of the present. To be absorbed in an activity, like a child becomes when playing a game or drawing, is to experience it fully, and thus to wring every last drop of enjoyment from it. Who ever thoroughly felt the exhilaration of a cross-country canter, or the melancholy beauty of a sunset, while their mind was worrying over an overdraft or an future job interview? Yoga teaches you to 'let go', to filter out distractions and just be.

## A note for nonbelievers

For atheists and agnostics, silent meditation is generally recommended as the better option: nonbelievers tend to feel uncomfortable with chants and prayers, however meaningless. Some would argue that nonbelievers are, in essence, closer to the transcendental state than the believer in that their spiritual consciousness is already clear of preconceived clutter.

# Chapter 3

# A Healthy Mind Equals
# a Healthy Body

## Dualism

Ever since the French philosopher Rene Descartes uttered 'I think therefore I am', we have been encouraged to identify ourselves with our conscious minds. We are good at chess, or have a ready wit, or can recite the kings and queens of England without prompting: our cleverness defines us. Descartes philosophy of Dualism prompted us to view our minds as distinct from our bodies: the former was an organ of reason and imagination, the latter an engine.

This did not happen to the same extent in the East, where a more holistic, integrated approach to the human mind and body, as in acupressure and acupuncture, which relate to the emotions as well as physical pressure points, was observed. In the West, however, medicine approached the body rather as mechanics approached the car. The symptoms of physical ailments were treated with little reference to what circumstances caused them to manifest themselves. Well, who would worry about how a car's tyre became punctured? Even worse perhaps, the human body was regarded as a series of separate parts, each to be treated by a different specialist, with little reference to the rest of the body.

This specialist approach has lead to enormous medical and surgical achievements. Many diseases have been virtually obliterated due to vaccines, diseased organs need no longer threaten life if a donor can be found, even in the field of mental illness, drugs have been developed that can suppress some of the distressing symptoms of conditions such as schizophrenia and manic depression.

The rub is that Western medicine has all too often ignored the fact that many complaints have their root in the mind. We call it psychosomatic if someone thinks they are ill just because they are depressed or out of sorts, but in fact we often become ill just because of those very feelings. Consider how different you feel on a Monday morning, when you don't want to get out of bed and go to work, and on a Saturday morning, when you can do exactly as you like. Of course, you feel ten times better on a Saturday. And we are not the only ones. Racehorses suffer from 'Monday Morning Sickness' too, becoming jittery and out of sorts immediately preceding a race. For an entire system of medicine, so advanced in many other ways, to have drawn a veil over this link between psyche and health is astonishing.

## Mind and body

Holistic (from the Greek holos, meaning 'whole') medicine has become increasingly popular in the West, especially amongst people who feel that the use of drugs can only help to a certain extent. The holistic approach regards the body and mind as one, where everything is connected to everything else, and nothing can happen to one part without everything else being affected. Thus, a patient of a holistic doctor might be asked about every area of his or her life, from how many cups of coffee a day are consumed to personal worries to where precisely that backache starts from. Illness is never specific to an area or organ.

Rather than prescribe drugs, a holistic doctor may prescribe a subtle change of lifestyle, some way of nudging the body back into gear. Furthermore, and perhaps most importantly, the patient is expected to participate in the healing process. Pharmacology has accustomed us to the idea that the patient's role is a passive one: we expect the doctor to do all the work, from diagnosis to selecting the right chemical. Holistic medicine is more honest in that it acknowledges it can only help to stimulate the body into healing itself, which in fact it is usually very capable of doing, given the right circumstances.

Meditation, frequently prescribed by holistic doctors, now has a stack of scientific evidence proving its enormous benefits to physical health.

## Stress

Stress is essential for a fulfilled life. Without it we would never try to do our best, and therefore never fulfil our potential. We would also need to be loveless to avoid it, friendless, holiday-less and opportunity-less. That does not sound like a recipe for happiness and health! But of course, too much can be disastrous, though how much is too much varies from one person to the next. Some people, often drawn to careers such as stock-market speculating, fast-moving business, sport or acting, absolutely thrive on high amounts of stress, and can often feel desolate when their working lives are over. For others, even relatively minor stresses, such as small money problems or forthcoming social events, can be very distressing. Boredom can also be very stressful, and many unemployed people are plagued by stress-induced problems.

Stress triggers off the 'fight or flight' response, which prepares the body for a burst of intense physical activity. The heart rate increases, more oxygen is pumped into the lungs, sugars are released into the blood stream to provide energy for the muscles, while digestion stops. This is the perfect state to be in if you are about to race off into the sunset or knock someone for six, but when negotiating a new bank loan or sitting in a fuming traffic jam, this response is less than useless. Your body can neither utilise this response, nor recover from it if the situation persists, as is the case with a rush-hour traffic jam. By the time you reach home you are more than ready for a drink, a cigarette, a row with someone – anything, to dispel that feeling of being 'wound up'.

Stress is also very damaging in the long term. Too much too often can result in hypertension (high blood pressure), asthma and migraine, and be a contributing factor in major diseases such as cancer and bronchitis. Research suggests that being over stressed can weaken the immune system, making you more susceptible to viral and other infections, and prolonging the recovery time. Even unborn babies can become the victims of stress if their mothers suffer from it while they are in the womb: such babies may develop more slowly, and have more emotional problems in later life than they would have had otherwise, through a tendency to cave in under pressure. Some estimate that as much as 70 per cent of illnesses are stress-related.

## Meditation and stress

Physical exercise can help to burn off a lot of this useless adrenaline, but a more lasting and effective antidote to stress is to tackle it at source – in the mind. The 'fight or flight' response is caused initially by thoughts that produce the response of fear, which then triggers off the biochemical reaction. Once this chain reaction starts it is very difficult to stop. Think of working to a deadline and realising that you are way behind schedule. The best thing you can do in this situation is get to it and try to make up for lost time. However, there is every possibility that your body is getting geared up for a boxing match: your heart is racing, your throat feeling tight, your palms sweating. Rather than setting to your work, you may be forced to sit back and let the stress reaction run its course. Which may very well leave you feeling even more stressed.

Suppose, however, you realise you are way behind schedule and instead of panicking, take control of your thought processes and thereby avoid the stress reaction. Regular meditation, because it enables you to recognise and therefore take charge of thought processes and how we are manipulated by them, can eventually enable you to take control, even in the most desperate of situations.

## Meditation and smoking

Although most smokers would love to be ex-smokers, most cannot make that transition because they fear the withdrawal symptoms, which often include depression, and because they feel that nicotine is essential to concentration and confidence. Like the slimming industry, companies that make products that are designed to help us give up smoking thrive on our yoyo-ing habits, but most over-the-counter products only help in the very short term.

Hypnosis has proved to be successful, but again only in the short term: after a few months, many people feel that they are just as vulnerable to temptation as they were the day after they gave up. Meditation is a very different way of going about it, because it is an internal, rather than external, approach, and goes right to the very heart of what prompts you to smoke in the first place. As the layers of who you thought you were, a clever person, a working mother, a good boy, start to melt away in your mind, leaving you with a clearer picture of yourself, you will also discover that you are not a 'die hard smoker' either. You will probably discover that you no more need a cigarette to get by than someone who has never smoked in his or her lives. Alongside this growing self-knowledge, which is also helping you to cope with a lot of the things you would instinctively light up in the face of, is a growing sensitivity to your own body. Eventually the desire to stop poisoning your body with nicotine will override your desire for a smoke. Studies of smokers who learned Transcendental Meditation showed that, after 24 months, 51 per cent had quit, and a significant number of them began the course without even a desire to stop smoking.

## Meditation and general wellbeing

Meditation, because it allows us to take stock of our inbuilt ideas about things, is also effective in combating health problems other than those that are stress-related. Negative emotions, such as suppressed anger, guilt or resentment, can be the starting point for digestive disorders, tension headaches and lowered immunity to infection. By contrast, visualisation techniques, such as visualising a diseased organ transforming into a healthy one, have proved remarkably successful in the treatment of cancer patients in the USA, as discussed in Dr Carl and Stephanie Simonton's book *Getting Well Again* (Bantam, 1986).

## Yoga and stress

Yoga also works effectively in the war to reduce stress because it requires absorption, diverting the mind from sources of anxiety. With regular practice you will begin to know your true self, not the one who attends meetings or has clocked up 10,000 air miles, but the essence of your being. This self-knowledge will lend you a deep-rooted confidence that will enable you to reorder your priorities in such a way that you are not permanently exhausted or missing out in the good things in life. It will help you to be assertive, but not aggressive, generous but not a doormat, and content without being complacent.

It can also bring about increased communion with, and respect for, your body, the desire for artificial stimulants lessens (after a few months of yoga, many smokers quit with relative ease), as does the tendency to eat whatever is convenient and skip exercise because you are too tired. Yoga will help you to be less tired as its ability to reduce anxiety will result in more restful sleep.

This new wellbeing is lasting, and can help to reverse the effects of even serious complaints, like heart disease, and can reduce the signs of aging. As one centenarian responded when asked the secret of long life: 'It's simple. Good food and no worries.'

# Chapter 4

# How to Begin

## Getting down to it

Having decided that meditation is something you would like to try, maybe for relaxation, maybe from more mystical motives, what is the next move? Before going on to look at meditation techniques, there are some basics to be considered. Posture is important, and hatha yoga will also be of great benefit in preparing for meditation.

In this chapter we shall look at both these essential elements.

## Posture

It is essential to adopt the correct position, not necessarily a sitting one, when meditating. Many practitioners of the art consider that the centuries-old seven-point posture is the most successful in helping to achieve a calm, clear state of mind and has yet to be bettered.

Others recommend the siddhasana, while many beginners opt for a simple cross-legged position (the easy posture), sitting in a chair (the Egyptian posture) or kneeling with the buttocks on the ankles (the Japanese, or thunderbolt, posture).

*Easy posture*

### Easy posture

Basically, this involves sitting cross-legged with both feet on the floor. The back should be straight but not tense and the stomach muscles relaxed. With the muscles of the lower back bearing the weight of the body and with the head, neck and trunk in line, the centre of gravity passes from the base of the spine right through the top of the head. The hands can either be resting lightly on the knees or held in the lap, either one on top of the other or clasped lightly.

### Siddhasana

Sitting on the floor with the back straight, stretch the legs out in front of you. Bend the left knee and, grasping the left foot with both hands, draw it towards the body until the heel is resting against the part of the lower body that lies between

*Siddhasana*

the anus and genitalia. Now draw the right foot towards the body until the heel is on the pubic bone. Tuck the toes of the right foot between the calf and the thigh of the left leg. Rest the hands, palms upwards on the knees. Siddhasana is sometimes called the perfect posture.

## Seven-point posture

1  If possible, try to sit with the legs crossed in the lotus position, or varja, with each foot placed sole upwards on the thigh of the opposite leg. To get into the lotus position loosen up with the exercises on pages 63–70 and then sit on the floor, legs stretched out in front of you. Now bend the right knee and, grasping the right foot with both hands, place it on top of the left thigh, heel pressing into the abdomen. Repeat the process with the left foot.

The soles should be turned up, with both knees on the ground.

If you cannot get into the full lotus position, try the half-lotus. Do the same seven exercises before stretching the legs out in front of you. Bend the left knee and put the left foot beneath the right thigh, as close to the buttock as you can get it. Now bend the right knee and put the right foot, sole up, on top of the left thigh. Keep both knees on the ground and the back straight. When you find that you can maintain this position comfortably throughout the session over a period of four or five weeks, you will be able to start trying the full lotus.

Sitting on a hard cushion will encourage you to keep the back straight and help you to sit for longer without getting irritating pins and needles in the legs and feet.

2   The hands should be held loosely on the lap about a centimetre below the navel, right hand on top of left, palms upwards, fingers aligned. Both hands should be slightly cupped so that the tips of the thumbs meet to form a triangle. The shoulders and arms should be relaxed. Never be tempted to press the arms against the body – they should be held a few centimetres away to allow the air to circulate which helps prevent feelings of drowsiness.

3   The back must be straight but relaxed. Try to imagine the spinal vertebrae as a pile of twopence pieces, delicately balanced one on top of the other that will crash to the ground if it is disturbed. A straight back encourages the energy to flow freely, and you will be able to meditate for longer and longer periods.

4   Many newcomers to meditation find it easier to concentrate with the eyes fully closed. This is not wrong, but it

is better to gaze downwards through slightly open eyes. Closed eyes encourage sleepiness and dreamlike images that mar meditation.

5   The jaw and mouth should both be relaxed, the teeth slightly apart, the lips lightly together.

6   Keep the tongue touching the palate just behind the upper teeth to reduce the flow of saliva and thus the need to swallow.

7   Bend the neck forward so that your gaze is directed to the floor in front of you. Don't drop it too low: this encourages sleepiness.

The seven-point position keeps the body and mind comfortable and free of tension. Beginners should not expect to be able to adopt it right away; it takes time to master.

*Seven-point posture*

## Seven simple exercises

Before trying to assume the lotus position, try these floor exercises to loosen the joints affected. Try to maintain a straight back and fixed head position throughout each exercise.

1  Stretch the legs straight out in front of you. Bend your right knee so that you can grasp the right ankle with both hands and put it on the left leg just above the knee so that the right foot is extending beyond the left leg. Keeping a firm grip on the ankle with the right hand, use the left hand to rotate the foot ten times in one direction and ten times in the other. Repeat the exercise with the left ankle and foot on the right leg.

2  Sitting in the same position as for the first exercise, put the right knee on the left leg as before and with both hands grasping the right ankle, lift it above the leg and shake the foot for twenty seconds. Repeat with the other leg.

3  Place the right foot on the left leg as before. Holding the foot in the left hand and wrapping the right hand around the leg at the ankle, lift the right leg as high as you can and make a large circle with the foot, drawing it close to the body at the top of the circle and pushing it away at the bottom. Repeat ten times before doing the same with the other leg.

4  With the palms of the hands flat on the floor behind and beyond the buttocks, bend the right knee and place the right foot as high up the left thigh as you can comfortably get it with the right knee as close to the ground as possible. Hold this position for a minute and then repeat with the other leg.

5  Supporting the body with the left hand flat on the floor

in the same position as for the last exercise, put the right foot as high up the left thigh as possible, place the right hand on the right knee and gently bounce for a count of ten. Repeat with the left leg.

6   Stretch the legs out in front of you and then slowly bend the knees outwards and draw the soles of the feet together. With the soles touching each other, bring the heels as close to the groin as possible and then, holding the toes with both hands, bounce the knees ten times, keeping them as close to the floor as possible. Hold for a count of ten.

7   Do the same as for the last exercise, but when the heels are as close to the groin as you can get them, put the hands on the knees and press them as far down to the floor as you can. Again, hold for a count of ten.

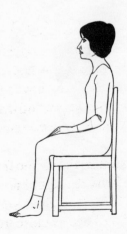

*The sitting position*

## The sitting position

Older people, or those with back problems who are unable to sit on the floor, can sit on a chair or on a low bench and lose themselves in meditation just as effectively as the more supple.

The ideal chair is one specially designed to encourage good posture: the chair is backless and has a slanted seat and knee rest. A straight-backed chair can also be used, in which case, sit on the front part of the seat with feet flat on the floor and legs slightly apart, the lower legs perpendicular to the floor.

It is inadvisable to meditate while sitting in an armchair or on the edge of a bed as the upholstery encourages you to slouch and become drowsy.

## Kneeling (the Japanese posture)

*Kneeling (the Japanese posture)*

Some people find this a convenient and comfortable position for meditation as it is easy to keep the spine straight. Simply kneel on the floor, keeping the knees together. Part the heels and bring the toes together so that you are sitting, straight-backed, on the insides of the feet with the hands on the knees.

## Lying flat

This position is called shavasanaor, the corpse position (*see* also page 228). Lie flat on the floor on a carpet, blanket or hard mattress. Part the legs a little and let the feet flop to the side. The arms should be slightly away from the body, hands on the floor, palms up.

Some teachers encourage their pupils to take up this position and relax for a short time before assuming one of the

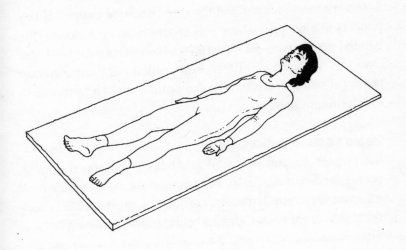

*Lying flat (shavasanor)*

other positions for the meditation session. Relaxing like this prepares the mind for the meditation proper. When you are in the corpse position, starting with the toes and working upwards to the brow, flex each muscle and shake each joint and then relax it before moving on to the next. When you have flexed the face muscles, go back to the beginning and tell each muscle to relax.

At first, some people feel self-conscious lying on their back and saying aloud, 'Toes relax!', 'Feet relax!' and so on. Their self-consciousness soon evaporates when they realise that the method works. When you are completely relaxed lie still for a few minutes, simply concentrating on your breathing before starting the meditation proper or assuming one of the other positions.

### Cupping the hands

Some teachers recommend that the hands be cupped if the pupil is in a posture where it is appropriate to do so. Right-handed people who decide to do this should cup the left hand over the right and, similarly, left-handed pupils should cup the right hand over the left, the point being to immobilise the dominant hand.

### Basic yoga exercises

In Chapter 13 you will find practical advice on the hatha postures, or asanas. It is very important to consider how intrinsic these are to meditation and it is most certainly useful at this point to introduce a regime that involves physical yoga exercise.

*Before you begin*

Before you begin, it is important to:

- Establish a convenient, regular time to practise.
- It is important not to have a full stomach.
- Wear comfortable and loose clothing.
- Use a clean, soft blanket or mat, thick enough to protect your spine and fit the length of your body.
- Perform each exercise slowly, carefully and mind-fully.
- Force and strain must be avoided.

Do not feel that a proper yoga session must include all the asanas. You will find some of them more difficult than others, and might want to leave them until you are more supple. Also, you may only have a short time slot for your regular sessions, in which case you should select a few and create a basic programme for yourself. This programme can be altered and added to at any time. There will also, inevitably, be periods when you do not feel inclined towards yoga practice at all. If this is so, then leave it. There is no point in forcing yourself, as yoga must be pleasurable to be effective. Some people leave their yoga for months at a time and then pick it up from where they left off. You might do the same, and it is important to remember that you can go back to it, and that you have not failed by letting it lapse.

The following are a series of suggested programmes to help you get started, but are not designed to be strictly adhered to. Yoga is a very personal thing, and not open to the dictates of others, including this book or a bossy yoga teacher!

*The warm-up*

It is vital to begin any yoga session with this basic warm-up routine of simple movements.

1   Standing in the tadasana (or mountain position, *see* page 178 for a fuller description of this position) keep your face forward, your feet together, your spine straight and your knees loose. Take a deep breath and as you exhale, slowly tilt your head to the left, your ear towards your shoulder. As you breathe in, raise your head back into the centre and tilt to the right upon the exhale. Repeat six times for each side. Concentrate on keeping these movements fluid and even. Sudden jerks could prove very painful.

Now lower your chin to your chest upon the exhale, raising it to the forward position on the inhale. Repeat three times,

*The mountain*

64

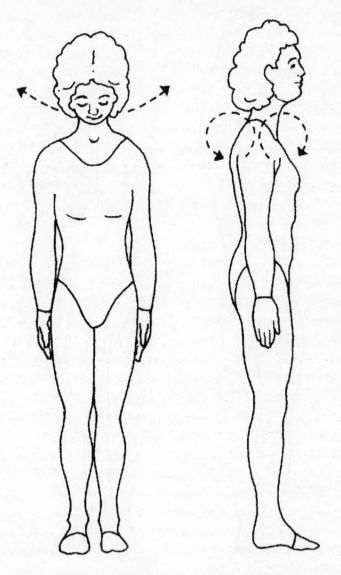

*Warm-up 1: Lower the chin*      *Warm-up 2: Lift shoulders*

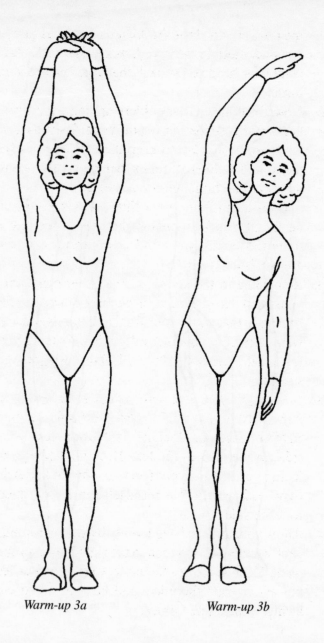

*Warm-up 3a*

*Warm-up 3b*

then lower your head backwards, again as you breathe out, and return to the upright upon the inhale. Try not to bend your head so far back that you squeeze your neck muscles.

2 Now lift both your shoulders up and back in a gentle backward rotation, as if you were describing a small circle in the air. Try to keep these circles as perfect as possible. Do this five times then repeat this exercise in a forward motion, again five times.

Both 1 and 2 are great little exercises for releasing neck and shoulder tension throughout the day, something those who work over computers or typewriters are particularly prone to.

3a Remaining in the tadasana, raise your hands up above your head. Keep your arms parallel and intertwine your fingers so that your hands form a bridge. Still facing forward, stretch your arms fully while keeping your feet flat on the ground. This will give your spine a good stretch.

3b Now return your left arm to your side, resting it palm downward on the side of your left thigh, keeping your right arm raised. Allow the right arm to lead you into a sideways stretch to the left. Keep your hips and chest facing forward and your feet flat. Now do a stretch to the right, leading with your raised left arm. Repeat three times for each side.

4 Allow your arms to hang loosely by your sides and swing gently to the left and then to the right in one slow movement. Keep your hips facing forward and your feet flat, but allow your shoulders and head to move with the swing. Repeat three times.

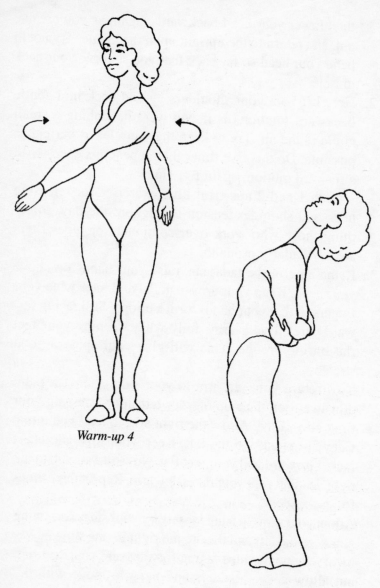

*Warm-up 4*

*Warm-up 5*

*Warm-up 6*

5 Now for a back stretch. Fold your arms behind your back, holding each elbow with the opposite hand. If this is too much of a strain, place both hands on the small of the back. Holding firmly with your hands, tuck in your buttocks, push your hips out and your head and shoulders back, so that your body forms a backward curve. Your weight should be centred on your heels. At first, you may find this uncomfortably precarious, in which case you may want to hold onto the back of a chair to steady yourself. Do not, however, transfer any of your weight from your heels as you may topple over backwards.

6 For the forward stretch, keep your arms folded behind

69

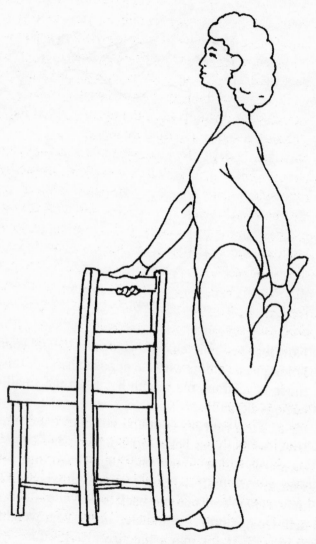

*Warm-up 7*

you or resting on the small of your back, and lean forwards towards the ground. Bend from the hips, keeping your back straight and your chin forward, until your torso forms a right angle with your legs. If you need the chair for balance, keep your hands on the back and gently step backwards until your back is straight. Stop the instant this becomes a strain, even if you feel that you have barely altered your position from the upright. Even the tiniest stretch is a step in the right direction.

7   Now for the legs. This exercise often requires the support of a chair back, which should be positioned by your right side. Facing forward, raise your right arm or hold the chair back, and bend your left leg so that your heel reaches your right buttock. Grip your ankle with your left hand and hold. Ideally the left knee should be facing downwards. This is a stretch that sprinters often do before a race, and is excellent for cooling down as well. Hold for a short period, or until it becomes uncomfortable, then repeat for the opposite leg.

8   Repeat step 3. Then give your legs a gentle shake and your arms a gentle shake.

### A beginner's regime

Before you begin, make sure that your mind is fully tuned into the idea of doing yoga. If your mind is elsewhere, try sitting down with your eyes closed and concentrating on clearing your mind. Try to hold each posture for a minute, and give yourself a ten second gap between each posture to relax and leave the posture behind. Think of how a gymnast, when performing on the beam, closes her eyes before moving onto the next part of her routine. She does this to clear her mind and focus her energies on the next movement; you should try to do the same.

1   Begin with the warm-up exercise above based on the tadasana. Remember to breathe correctly and to avoid straining as you move into the stretches. Take your time with each of the eight steps and give your arms and legs a gentle shake at the end. You are now back in the tadasana pose, so close your eyes, breathe in deeply and, as you exhale, clear your mind in preparation for the next move.

2   Move now into the tree posture (vrksasana, *see* also page 185), the praying position. Locate a spot on which to fix your gaze and remember to distribute your weight evenly across the sole of your foot. Always begin with your right side, and do so for all exercises. There is no mystic reason for this, but it helps you to know where you are in your routine, and prevents you dithering about which side to begin with, which can be surprisingly stressful. Aim to hold the pose for 20–30 seconds

*Beginner's regime 2: the tree*

*Beginner's regime 3: the cobra*

each side. If you find that you keep toppling over then use a chair to hold onto lightly. Sometimes even knowing that the chair is there, should you need it, can be all you require to maintain your upright position. Concentrate on the idea of yourself as a tree, with your feet as the roots that lead into the ground, and you will increase your sense of security in this asana. Once both your feet are back on the ground, close your eyes, and get ready for the next move.

3  Lie down on your front in preparation for the cobra (bhuhanjasana, *see* also page 186). With your hands under your shoulders, lift yourself back slowly upon the inhale until your arms are straight. Think of your vertebrae as like the bones of a snake, bending backwards in unison. Remember to keep your hips and legs in contact with the floor. Try to hold this posture for a minute, and then slowly lower yourself to the floor. Take a few seconds to relax and then repeat the exercise, this time increasing the stretch a fraction. Do not, however, bend so

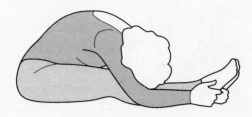

*Beginner's regime 4: the forward bend* (paschimottanasana)

much that it becomes unpleasant. Again, lower yourself to the floor and take your usual ten second break.

4   To counteract the stretch of the cobra, your next move is the forward bend (paschimottanasana, *see* also page 188), which will allow the muscles of your abdomen and chest to contract. Roll gently round so that your are sitting upright, with your legs stretched out straight in front of you. On the inhale, bend your upper body forward from the hips. If you cannot reach your toes, then grasp your ankles or even knees. If this bend strains your back then you might want to try using a scarf to help you. Holding each end of the scarf, loop it over your feet so that you can pull yourself into the forward stretch. This will help to increase the flexibility of your back and soon you should be able to dispense with this aid. This posture should induce a calmness. If it doesn't then you are either trying too hard or not concentrating. Aim to hold the pose for a minute, and then relax, giving yourself a moment to come out of it mentally.

*Beginner's regime 5: the spinal twist*

5   Now you are ready for the spinal twist (*see* also page 193), which begins as with the previous exercise, by sitting upright with your legs straight out in front of you. Keep your head and spine erect by imagining a piece of string attached to your crown, pulling your slightly upwards towards the ceiling. Begin by placing the right leg over the left leg so that your right foot rests on the outside of the left knee. Allow your left hand to support you by placing it behind you at the centre of the spine, but don't lean into it. As you twist your upper body to the left, remember that it is your shoulders leading this movement, not your head. Hold for a minute and then repeat for the other side. This should iron out any twinges in the small of your back.

6   Once you have taken your ten second break, prepare for the shoulder stand (sarvangasana, *see* also page 223). If you are menstruating or have heart problems, leave this asana out and move onto the next stage. Before you begin, ensure that your neck and shoulders are going to be

*Beginner's regime 6: the shoulder stand* (sarvagasana)

protected from the floor by a folded blanket or mat. Lie back with your arms stretched out by your sides and your palms flat on the floor. Allow your knees to rise up and lift the lower body into the air, and your centre of gravity to shift to your shoulders. Your weight should not be centred on your neck or the hands now supporting your lower back. Your legs should be straight and in alignment with your upper body. In short, your bottom should not be sticking out! Hold for a minute and then slowly unroll yourself onto the floor.

*Beginner's regime 7: the fish* (matyasana*)*

7   To release any tensions that may have built up in your neck and shoulder during the previous exercise, you are now going to do the fish (matyasana, *see* also page 195). Begin on your back and gently arch your back keeping your buttocks firmly in contact with terra firma. Arch your back till your head can be lowered back to rest on its crown, and redistribute your weight so that your head and buttocks are supporting it equally. It is very important that you do not feel that your head is wedged into position. When you are ready, bring your hands up to chest level so that the palms meet in the praying position. Relax into this posture and hold for a minute before lowering yourself down using your arms as support. Close your eyes and give your mind a chance to clear.

8   Now stand up and place your feet at least a shoulders'

width apart in preparation for the triangle (*see* also page 183). Begin by raising your right arm so that it brushes against your ear, with your left arm flat against the outside of your left thigh. Take a deep breath and pull yourself over to the left, allowing your left hand to slip down the thigh towards the ankle. Keep your hips facing forward. When you are stretched as far as you can, hold the pose before raising yourself gently upright. Repeat for

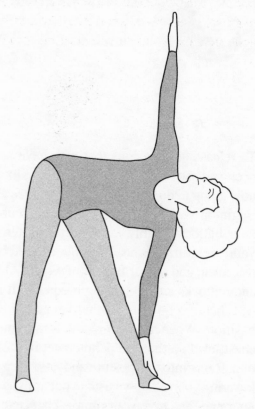

*Beginner's regime 8: the triangle*

the other side, and then repeat the exercise three times. This may seem a lot, written down on paper, but if you concentrate fully on what you are doing, you will not notice the time passing.

9   Now move into the thunderbolt position (*see* also page 229), remembering to keep your back and head upright. Place your hands on your knees and take a deep breath, breathing from the diaphragm. Hold this pose for a minute. Keep your eyes closed but visualise yourself sitting here so peacefully and still, like a living statue. Take a moment or two to come out of this pose.

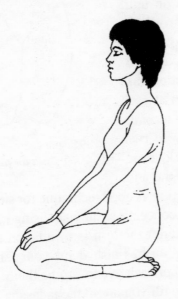

*Beginner's regime 9: the thunderbolt*

10 An important part of every yoga session should be the workout of the face, so prepare yourself for the cow-face

posture (*see* also page 230). Link your arms behind your back, take a deep breath and visualise that giant clock face in front of you. Without moving your head or furrowing your brow, look up at twelve o'clock and hold for a few seconds. Move to one o'clock, two o'clock and so on until you come right round to twelve again. Now repeat the process in an anti-clockwise direction, taking care to stop at each hour for a few seconds. It is very easy to rush round the clock, especially going in the anti-clockwise direction. A good technique for slowing yourself down is to concentrate on visualising each number in turn, and where exactly it is in relation to the other numbers. When you are finished, rub your palms together and cup them over each eye to soothe them.

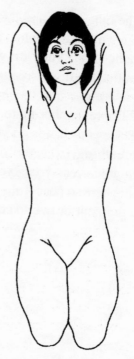

*Beginner's regime 10: the cow face*

11 Slowly stand up till you are in the tadasana once again. Take a deep breath, close your eyes and think of yourself standing on the top of a high mountain. Can you smell the cold clean air? Take a series of deep breaths and enjoy the sensation of being upright, of your body natu-

rally balancing itself. Hold for a minute, before relaxing.

12 The final stage, as with all yoga sessions is the corpse posture. Lie down on your back, and let yourself be heavy into the floor. Close your eyes and be on that beach, with the soft sand underneath you. Begin with your toes, flexing and relaxing each area in turn. For the relaxation benefits of this posture to work, it is important not to mentally 'hurry yourself up' so that you can get on with making the tea or whatever. This is your time, you deserve it,

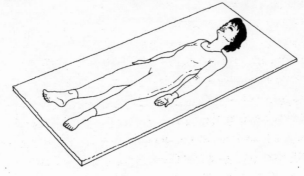

*Beginner's regime 12: the corpse (lying flat)*

so sink into it as you would a wonderful hot bath at the end of an exhausting day.

If you are wondering, as you read through this suggested programme, how on earth you are supposed to remember it all, then don't worry, you are not the first person to wonder. Some people like to read out their routine into a cassette and play it back to themselves as they practise. The only drawback with this is that the pace is dictated by the voice, unless you are near enough to the tape-deck to press pause when you feel that your voice is being a little hasty or you wish to hold a pose for a little longer. Alternatively, you can try to memorise the routine and draw yourself a series of twelve diagrams, to be placed somewhere visible, to prompt you as you go along. You will find, however, that you soon know instinctively what comes next, though don't repeat the same routine so often that you become bored with it. Alternate your sessions, adding in new postures or changing the order. Remember, of course, to counter each forward stretch with a backward stretch and to repeat side stretches on both sides.

# Chapter 5
# The Meditation Session

Once you are sitting comfortably in the seven-point posture, siddhasana, or whichever of the other recommended positions suits you best, spend a minute or two settling your body and mind, deciding which meditation you will do and how long you will meditate.

Some meditators prostrate themselves three times before settling down to meditate, believing that this counteracts pride, which is a barrier to effective meditation. Egotism and self-absorption only serve to hinder our perceptions, rendering other people and the outside world disproportionately unimportant compared to our external (as opposed to inner) selves. Though self-importance may of course be a shield for deep personal unease, it is essential to let it go if the meditation is to be successful.

Now run through your thoughts. Set your goals. Why are you about to meditate? What do you hope to achieve by it? The more motivated you are and the clearer your goal, the more successful the meditation is likely to be.

Many people take up meditation simply to relax, though some are so stressed that they need to learn to relax before they can meditate. Try to think of your meditation as a gift of time to yourself. Many people, particularly women, find to their amazement that they very rarely allow themselves time simply 'to be'. Remember that, no matter what the demands on your time, you can afford fifteen minutes out of a day, especially such a beneficial fifteen minutes. You will return to the world with renewed vigour and a cleared mental desk. In fact, with just the state of mind a newspaper editor would kill for when she's forcing back deadlines and (invariably) large jugs of black coffee.

Some meditation regulars even find that they need less sleep than before they took it up. Like catnappers (a famous example being Baroness Thatcher who slept only four hours a night, but sustained herself throughout the day with a series of twenty-minute catnaps), they grab moments of rest during the bustle of the day, and therefore finish up much less worn out than they would have been otherwise.

Often, when people become more experienced at meditation their aims become more far-reaching, and they feel themselves drawn to the more mystical side of meditation – the search for an understanding of the nature of reality. The deeper they search, the calmer, happier and more satisfied they become. Some go too far! They assume a smug, self-satisfied attitude that is not just off-putting to others but defeats the whole object of the exercise.

## Which technique?

There are many different methods of meditation. Some have been handed down from generation to generation for thousands of years and remain in their pure form. Others have been adapted to suit current circumstances. Deciding which of them is right for you can be quite bewildering, but bear in mind that the techniques are not ends in themselves: they are the motorway on which the journey to meditation moves.

The best technique for you is the one with which you feel most comfortable.

## Experiment

Start perhaps with breath-awareness techniques, which are the simplest. Many people go no further. Others experiment with different techniques until they find another method they prefer or they come back to breath awareness. Despite the extravagant claims made by the followers of their own particular favourite, there is no technique that is better than any of the others.

Try not to decide on a method after just one session. Give it a trial run over a week or two, jotting down the frame of mind you were in before you went into meditation and how you felt when you came out of it. At the end of the trial period, try and see if that particular method has improved the quality of your life. If it has, and you feel comfortable with it, stick to it, for by using a method that suits you and making it part of your life you will make much faster progress than if you dabble in one and then move on to another just for experiment's sake.

## Proper breathing

This is vital to proper meditation. Generally, you should breathe in at your normal rate through the nose. Don't be tempted to force yourself to breathe more deeply or more slowly than usual. You will probably find that the deeper you meditate, the slower and more deeply you will breathe.

A technique called bellows breathing, or bhastrika pranayama, is recommended by experienced meditators to quieten the mind before meditation proper begins. The prac-

tice involves breathing in and out rapidly by forcing the abdominal muscles to expand and contract rapidly. It takes a
great deal of practice to breathe properly in this way, and
even those who have mastered the technique should never
try it until at least three hours after eating, and they should
eat nothing for at least half an hour afterwards.

It should be noted that breathing in this way can produce
dizziness and nausea and should never be practised by pregnant women, anyone with hyper- or hypotension or with heart
or lung problems. It is best learned from a teacher than from
the pages of a book such as this.

### The time . . .

There are no set rules as to how often you should meditate
– some people meditate every day, others find just once a
week suits them. It doesn't matter, as long as you meditate
regularly, but remember that if you let too long a period
elapse between sessions you will be as out of shape,
meditatively speaking, as ballet dancers would be if they
didn't go to a class regularly. There will certainly be days
when you are due to meditate when it is the last thing you
want to do, but try anyway, even if only for a few minutes.
It is best not to meditate for at least two hours after eating
a meal.

Some people greatly enjoy meditation in the morning, just
as the day is beginning. A sense of peace and inner calm is,
to some, the ideal way to start out. Others prefer the evening,
because they can look forward to it during the day, and it
helps them to relax and throw off their working cares, and
therefore fully enjoy their evening. Still others prefer a meditation in the middle of the day, which is particularly benefi-

cial for those who work long, erratic hours in stressful jobs. A fifteen-minute meditation can be just the boost you need for a productive and efficient afternoon, which in turn will make you feel good.

### . . . and the place

If you have a large house, reserve a room specially for meditation, but if space is a problem, set aside a corner of a suitable room. Put a mat on the floor close to a table or bench for books you may need for your meditation, or for the picture or image on which you are going to focus your thoughts.

Make sure the area is clean, quiet and as pleasing as you can make it so that it is somewhere you will look forward to being in. Make sure, too, that you tell your family you don't want to be disturbed while you are meditating.

Some find that the more a place is used for meditation, the more peaceful it becomes. After all, churches have particularly tranquil atmospheres whereas few would expect to feel comfortable closing their eyes and meditating in an airport lounge. The atmosphere can be enhanced with sound: you could play a cassette of natural sounds such as the sea or bird song, or a Gregorian chant, and soft, indirect lighting is very comforting. Colours too are also important: bright red will keep you alert but also distract you from your meditations, a gentle blue or white will match your calm.

Some people burn candles and incense sticks. If you think they will help you to meditate or make the room more conducive to meditation by all means follow their example. Remember that to meditate effectively you must be as relaxed as possible.

## The meditation object

This is something on which the attention can focus and on which it may rest, ideally for the full session, although in practice this rarely happens as even experienced meditators may find their attention wandering at some time or other (*see* Problems below), but the meditation object is always there to come back to.

The object may be something to look at – a flower, a candle, a religious icon or a mandala or yantra, symbols specially designed for meditation. It may be something you can listen to – a cassette recording the sound of the sea or a running river or bird song, for example. It can be as everyday as the ticking of the clock or as esoteric as the tinkling of temple bells.

Many meditators use a mantra, a word or phrase repeated again and again either out loud or mentally.

The meditation object can even be your own breath.

These are all discussed in more detail in Chapters 8 and 9.

## Problems

Even the most practised meditators may experience difficulties, so beginners should not be put off if they find it hard to get into a meditative state of mind or to maintain concentration.

One of the most common problems is mental excitement. The mind becomes restless and the attention is continually distracted. Sometimes we are unable to banish nagging problems from our thoughts – for example, job security, paying household bills, health worries. If we are in a particularly good frame of mind, we may unintentionally recall things that have made us smile – a new friendship, an enjoyable conversation, even a television programme we have enjoyed.

In our everyday lives we let our minds jump from thought to thought, from worry to worry, so mental wandering is a deeply ingrained habit and, like any habit, is difficult to give up. One popular way of overcoming it is to concentrate on breathing, which has a very calming effect on one's state of mind.

Be patient. It takes time and practise to learn how to slow and control the mind. Don't give up. Even St Teresa of Avila, a very experienced meditator, encountered difficulties. When she overheard a novice at her convent remark that it must be wonderful to 'be like Sister Teresa' and not be bothered by distractions during prayer and meditation, she surprised the girl by saying, 'What do you think I am, a saint?'

Another common problem is drowsiness. When we are in a completely relaxed frame of mind, it is all too easy to drop off. If you start to feel sleepy while meditating, make sure that you are sitting up straight and your head is not bent too far forward. If you are meditating with your eyes closed, open them and meditate with the gaze directed at the floor just in front of you. If you are meditating in a centrally heated room, turn down the heating or open a window to freshen the air. Increasing the amount of light in the room can also help you to stay awake.

**Physical tension**

Any physical discomfort makes effective meditation difficult. Often such discomfort is a physical manifestation of mental turmoil – it could be an unresolved problem or worry, or something that has made you angry. So if your meditation is disrupted by physical discomfort for no obvious reason, then try to recognise any such problems and settle it in meditation. Another reason why you may find yourself in some physical discomfort is that, due to your heightened state of awareness, you have become more conscious of your bodily sensations. Just as, for example, after a long written exam, you suddenly discover that your hands are cramped and your neck hurts. Thus, when meditation lifts you from the tramlines of your everyday thought patterns, you may notice aches and tensions that were hitherto concealed by your preoccupations.

One way of getting rid of physical tension is to focus your attention for a moment on each part of the body in turn, starting with the head and working downwards, making a conscious effort to make it relax. You can do this at the start of the session or during it if need be.

Deep, slow breathing can also prove tremendously helpful. Concentrate as hard as you can, and as you breathe out, try to imagine the pain or tension evaporating.

Meditation can also be used for pain management, whether it be to ease the discomfort of a headache or cope with the painful aftereffects of chemotherapy. Some people use the pain as a focus for their meditation, first locating and feeling it in all its intensity, and then picturing it as an entity that is something distinct from their inner self. This way the pain can be felt to be not intrinsic to that person, not as strong as the person, conquerable by the person.

As well as benefiting the sufferer in easing his or her discomfort, meditation can also be very empowering. Having once felt at the mercy of a disease, many people feel that they have regained control of their own body through meditation.

## Long-term benefits

Try not to expect too much too quickly. In fact, it is far better, to begin with, not to have any expectations at all. Otherwise these expectations could put pressure on you while you meditate, and this will inevitably thwart any bids for inner calm. However, don't think that because you have been meditating every day for a week or two and feel absolutely no benefit, meditation is not working for you. It can take months, sometimes years, for positive changes to manifest themselves, and even when they do, they can happen over such an extended period you may not be aware of the difference regular meditation is making to you. Others, however, will certainly realise that something about you has changed for the better. You will seem calmer, less flustered by petty events, more open and sensitive to other people. Many therapists practice meditation for the very reason that it enables them to be still inside and therefore capable of giving their full attention to a client.

## Breaking the spell

Avoid coming out of meditation too quickly, for if you do, most of the benefits you have achieved will be lost. Once you have finished meditating remain in your meditative position for a minute or two and then slowly stretch, catlike, quietly reflecting on how good you now feel – calmer and better equipped to cope with everyday living. Instead of acting impulsively or emotionally, you will be more thoughtful and better equipped to deal with life's problems.

# Chapter 6

# Breathing Techniques

## Awareness of breath

Correct abdominal breathing lies at the heart of all kinds of meditation. In 'awareness of breath' meditation, breathing itself is the object of the meditation. Such meditation is held in the highest regard among Buddhists, Hindus and Taoists, all of whom believe in it not just as a means of inducing peace of mind but also of encouraging physical and mental health.

Breathing awareness can also be used as a prelude to another form of meditation. If this is to be the case, five minutes or so will calm the nerves and focus and still the mind, putting it in a receptive mood for the session proper.

Awareness of breath meditation techniques are ideal for the novice meditator because they are entirely natural and most people feel quite comfortable with them. The techniques simply involve being aware of the breath as it enters and leaves the body.

Sit motionless in any of the postures you find comfortable, remembering to keep the back, head and neck in perfect balance, and begin to think about your breathing, becoming aware of each intake of breath, the pause, the expulsion of stale air from the lungs, the pause, the next breath.

Your attention will wander. Don't be put off; bring it back to the object of your meditation and start again on the next inhalation.

It is not unusual for the pattern of breathing to change during meditation. At first, when you may be feeling a little self-conscious, you may find that you are holding each breath for longer than usual, but as the meditation proceeds you should find that breathing becomes smoother and deeper, or it may become shallow and slow. Don't be concerned by this. As you concentrate on your breathing and lose yourself in the meditation, the body establishes a rate of breathing that is right for that particular time.

There are several methods for encouraging attention to focus on the breath. None of them is better than any of the others. Try them all, and if you are happier with one over the rest, stick with it. Naturally they all require you to adopt a suitable posture and choose an appropriate place. One newcomer to breath awareness meditation decided to try it in a stuffy underground train. He closed his eyes, put his thoughts in order, began to breathe in and out as he had learned . . . and was woken by the guard when the train reached the terminus many stops past his own.

## The simplest methods

Take up a comfortable posture. You may shut your eyes to aid concentration, but it is better to keep them half open. Breathe as naturally as you can, counting either each inhalation or exhalation up to ten, and repeat this for twenty minutes. Counting is an aid to concentration and helps to prevent the mind from wandering.

Some people find it helps if they focus their attention on

the tip of the nose or the inside of the nostrils as the breath enters and leaves the body. Others use the movement of the abdomen as the focus of their attention.

## Mindfulness of breathing meditation

'A monk having gone to the forest, to the foot of a tree, or to an empty place, sits down cross-legged, keeps his body erect and his mindfulness alert. Just mindful he breathes in and mindful he breathes out.'

Thus did the Suddha advocate to his followers mindfulness of breathing meditation, also called 'following the breath'.

According to this widely practised method of meditation, the abdomen or nose is the focus of attention, which is a development of basic awareness of breath meditation which many people find unsatisfying after a month or two.

There is no counting in mindfulness of breath meditation, rather it is the flow of breath in and out on which the mind is concentrated. To practise it, sit comfortably in any of the prescribed positions with the eyes closed and breathe in and out quite naturally, focusing the attention either on the abdomen or the nose.

If it's the abdomen, become aware of the pause in breathing at the limit of each sea-swell-like rise and fall of the abdomen. If it's the nose, concentrate on the nostrils where the flow of inhaled and exhaled air can be felt.

You are certain to find at first that your attention wanders even if you have been successfully practising counting the breath meditation for some time. When you realise that your attention has meandered, simply return it to the abdomen or nose and continue the meditation.

As you give in to the seductive rhythm of your abdomen as it rises and falls or your sensation of the inflow or outflow of air in the nostrils, your breathing will become smoother and much quieter as the meditation deepens.

Try to avoid controlling your breathing in any way. This can be difficult. Watching the breath without trying to interfere with it seems simple, but it takes some practice for the mind to become used to the fact that you are trying to surrender yourself completely to the spontaneous flow of the breath. Beginners usually find that their breathing becomes uneven, quickening and slowing for no apparent reason. They should not worry, for in time the breath settles to its own rhythm.

Many of those who practise following the breath meditation find it helps if they make themselves aware of the journey of each breath from the moment it enters the nostril to the moment it is expelled. Others picture an aura of energy and light just in front of the forehead. With each breath some of the power is taken into the body and the meditator focuses on its journey deep into the body.

Most of the faiths or religions that advocate breathing meditation have their own techniques. Zen Buddhists, for example, sometimes imagine that a ball of lead drops slowly through the body with each breath-making the stale deoxygenated air fall out.

Many have their own methods of dealing with the inevitable distractions. Some Buddhist teachers encourage their pupils to use the distractions themselves as the objects of meditation temporarily. These thoughts will eventually dissolve and mindfulness of breathing meditation can be resumed.

## Yoga breathing

The way that we breathe is inextricably linked to our sense of wellbeing and our emotions. When we are frightened or very stressed we start to take very quick, shallow breaths and when we are very relaxed, or asleep, our breathing becomes much slower and deeper. Both these processes are entirely involuntary, caused by the body reacting to signals sent out by the brain. The problem with shallow breathing, while doing us no harm if sustained only for a short period, is that if it affects our general breathing pattern, as it can do when we are constantly under stress, our whole health will suffer. Shallow breathing means that we are using only a fraction of the lungs' capacity, and failing to supply our muscles and organs, via the blood, with sufficient quantities of fresh oxygen. This results in those muscles and organs being unable to function properly.

Try taking a really deep breath right now. Do you feel as if you are taking in a lot more air than usual? And do you suddenly feel more alert than you did a moment ago? The fact is, lack of oxygen in the blood stream makes us feel tired and prone to headaches. Thus when we feel tired, we yawn. A yawn is the body's way of sucking in more air, just as a thermostat triggers an extra burst of energy in a heating system when the temperature falls below the set level.

Correct breathing can make a huge difference to the way we feel. A few deep breaths can help to ease off a mild case of indigestion. It can wake us up and help us to sleep. It can even help to lower anxiety as focusing on long, slow breaths coerces the mind into slowing itself down too. Recently it has been discovered that learning to play the bagpipes, which requires a great deal of deep breathing to generate enough air, can help to alleviate asthma. This is because the practice of deep breathing increases lung capacity and thereby helps the sufferer to take control of, rather than be controlled by, their breathing patterns.

## Pranayama

Yoga breathing is called pranayama. 'Prana' means 'breath of life' and 'ayama' means 'interval' so combined it means 'the interruption of breath'. Breath, as well we all know, is the stuff of life. Without it we die. Yogis regard breath as much more than the element oxygen; to them it is the force that connects us with the life-force of the universe. Correct breathing unblocks the channels of energy that run through the body (*see* The Chakras, page 245), and balances the negative and positive forces, the masculine and feminine, yin and yang, within us. Please note that all pranayama exercises, unless otherwise stated, should be done with your mouth shut so that you breathe through your nose. Before beginning it is best to take a shower, clear your sinuses and rinse out your mouth. As with the asanas, do not undertake these exercises within two hours of a heavy meal, or an hour of a light snack.

## Holding the breath

Imagine you are standing at the kerb of a street, cars haring past in both directions. Suddenly you see a football bounce onto the road and, an instant later, a small child run out after it, heedless to the speeding traffic. You hear the squeal of breaks and, in the vital seconds that follow, the world seems to go silent. People in such circumstances have described performing incredible feats of quick thinking and daring without feeling as if it were them actually doing it. 'Something took over', 'I seemed to be watching myself doing it' they might recall as they lie gasping for breath by the roadside, clutching the terrified child. That instant of silence is what is referred to as a 'heart-stopping moment'. In such instances, where fast action is required, we feel as if our heart has literally stopped breathing and some superhuman force has taken control. We become able to do things that normally lie outwith our capabilities. In fact, our heart has not stopped, and no exterior force has moved in on us. The sudden sensation of stillness is caused by our holding our breath, and by doing so, we are enabled to focus our minds totally on the task in hand.

Psychologists have estimated that we use only about 20 per cent of our brain capacity at any given time, simply because we do not know how to fully tap into its resources. The exceptional Albert Einstein is guessed to have utilised as much as 40 per cent, and think how much he achieved in so doing. Of course, holding your breath is not going to turn you into Einstein, but the involuntary action of the body certainly stimulates the brain into given an above-average performance. It enables us to swerve the car out of harm's way at a split-second's notice, police negotiators to talk someone into handing over a weapon in a highly volatile situation and examinees to answer questions correctly in situations on which their futures depend. Without this inbuilt system we would panic, our minds racing hither and thither without settling on a course of action, our bodies become unable to act.

Holding the breath is a means of focusing the mind and, as such, is a very important part of pranayama, especially in training for meditation, which will be dealt with in the following chapter. It cannot be over-stressed that yogic breath holding is not the same as holding your breath in preparation for a underwater dive, or an endurance test. Under no circumstances should it ever be forced or uncomfortable, and it should be avoided by anyone suffering from hypertension (high blood pressure) or a heart problem.

A simple breath retention exercise to try begins with sitting in the thunderbolt or Egyptian position, with your hands resting lightly on your knees and your eyes closed. Inhale slowly and deeply, but without any sensation of straining. When you have fully inhaled, count to two in your head, and slowly exhale. You should not need to gasp outwards unless you have breathed in too forcefully. Repeat several times, but stop if it becomes unpleasant. Gradually you will be able to build up your breath retention to 60 or even 90 seconds, but avoid feeling as if your must 'better your record'. You are not, repeat not, training for the Olympic underwater swimming team.

### The alternate nostril breath

This is a classic pranayama technique and helps to restore the yin-yang balance. The fact is, we rarely breathe through both nostrils so this exercise evolved to ensure that we learn how to.

Begin by sitting in one of the sitting asanas as before. Using one of the fingers of your right hand, ideally the third, press the right nostril shut. Breathe in, keeping the right nostril closed, so that your left nostril is forced to do all the work. Now press the left nostril shut as well, using the thumb of your right hand. Count to sixteen, retaining that breath.

Release your right nostril and exhale gently. Now repeat the exercise, beginning with the left nostril closed. Repeat this process five times, but remember to do the exercise calmly and slowly.

This exercise is very good for clearing the sinuses and speeding up the expulsion of phlegm.

### The buzzing bee

This is a very soothing exercise, ideal for calming down at the end of a busy, noisy day. Sitting comfortably, allow your facial muscles to relax and shape your lips as if you were about to blow into a flute. Your hands should be resting lightly on your knees. Now close your eyes and imagine yourself sitting on a lawn on a summer's afternoon. Feel the heat of the sun on your face and smell the warm earth and the flowers. Breathe gently and deeply, and then, on an exhale, breathe out through your lips making a steady 'Hmmmm' sound until all your breath has gone. Inhale deeply and repeat several times. This will create a gentle vibration throughout your body and remind you of the sleepy drone of a bumble bee moving from flower to flower. Give yourself a moment or two to 'come to' before opening your eyes.

### The bellows breath

Normally, when we breathe in, we do so forcefully, while breathing out is the automatic, passive reaction. A pair of bellows, on the other hand, fills up with air of its own accord and external force must be exerted to pump the air out. The bellows breath mimics this process.

The best way to perform the bellows breath is standing up with your feet pointing outward, your legs slightly apart and your knees bent. Your upper body should be tilted slightly forward, bending from the hips, and your head in alignment with your back, your face looking down. Hold onto the tops of your thighs, palms down, with your elbows bent away from the body. If this reminds you of the postures struck by rosy-cheeked peasants having a jolly good laugh in medieval depictions of country fairs, then well and good. Mimicking the action of a deep laugh will show you exactly how this exercise works. Take a deep breath and then quickly eject the air through your nostrils, as if you were having a long, silent guffaw. You will notice that the air seems to flood back into your lungs without any effort on your part. Try this again. Your inward breath should take longer than your outward breath, but take care to avoid forcing the breath out for longer than is comfortable or feels natural, as this is counterproductive. You are not trying to recreate the ghastly sensation of being winded by a blow to the stomach.

Repeat this for up to ten times; the sound of your breathing should resemble that of an angry bull preparing to charge! If you feel at all dizzy or uncomfortable, then stop and return to normal breathing. Just as a good hearty laugh makes you feel more alive and alert, so too will the bellows breath as it stimulates the brain. The doctors are quite right when they say that laughter is the best medicine.

*The cooling breath*
This is not dissimilar to the actions of cats and dogs when they stick out their tongues to cool themselves on a hot day, and it is very effective when your body feels overheated, whether through illness, hot weather or central heating.

Sit comfortably and stick out your tongue a little way (though not to the degree that you would for the lion posture; your tongue should not feel stretched). Curl the outer sides of your tongue inwards to form a funnel. Some people cannot 'roll' their tongues in this way, but even a slight inward curve will be effective. Close your eyes and breathe in along this funnel. It should feel lovely and cool. Retain this breath for a few seconds, bringing your tongue in and closing your mouth. Exhale slowly through your nostrils. Think of the process as a cooling system, bringing in cool air and taking hot air out in a continuous cycle. Repeat three times.

### The victorious breath (ujjayi)
To do this exercise, you must learn to partially close your glottis. This is located at the top of the windpipe between the vocal chords. We naturally close and open our glottis during speech, and most noticeably so when we utter a glottal stop. A glottal stop is a plosive speech sound we make when, for instance, we pronounce the word 'butter' but drop the 'tt' sound. Try it and you will hear a gentle sound emanating from your throat; this is the sound of the glottis closing and opening. In ujjayi you seek to make this noise continuous by controlling the breath and keeping it steady.

Begin by standing in the tadasana and lock your chin into the jugular notch. This chin lock is called the jalandhara and assists in the process of retaining the breath. Now breath in slowly and deeply, hold for perhaps five seconds, and release in a slow, controlled manner, keeping your glottis partially shut. If the sound wavers, then your exhalation is unsteady. Repeat five times, and, if you concentrate, the sound will become steadier.

This exercise is called the 'victorious breath' because it is said to instil courage. It will certainly remind you of an animal gearing itself up to go on the rampage! It is also good for circulation and clearing the nose and throat, which, in a polluted world, is a victory in itself.

### The cleansing breath (kapalabhati)

To begin, sit in the thunderbolt or half-lotus position and take a few moments to relax. Breath through your nose and from your diaphragm. When you are ready, take a deep inward breath through your nostrils and then exhale sharply, in a single gust, by contracting your diaphragm. Make sure that you exhale all the air from your lungs. It will sound a bit like a sneeze. Now repeat this process up to ten times, and then relax.

This is a good exercise for clearing the sinuses and boosting the blood circulation.

Another way to do achieve this cleanliness is to stand up straight, with your feet slightly apart. Take a long deep breath and swing your arms above and beyond your head, keeping them straight. Your whole body should be curved backwards to form the shape of a shallow backward C. Now bring your arms round towards your feet in a single movement, and, as you do so, exhale sharply by contracting the diaphragm. Again, make sure that you get all the air out of your lungs in this single exhalation. This is more vigorous exercise than the previous one, so do not attempt to repeat it ten times. About three to five times is more than sufficient.

Perhaps one of the best ways to feel that you have really given your lungs a good clean is to practise breathing exercises beside the sea or a river or stream. These areas are rich in negative ions which help us to feel very refreshed and rejuvenated. Areas where there is a lot of pollution are filled with positive ions which tend to make us feel tired. The last ten years has seen the introduction of ionisers into some workplaces. These machines convert positive ions into negative ones, and the workforce from a sleepy lot to a wide-awake crew. Or at least, so the theory goes, though many people have found them to be enormously beneficial.

## Control over responses

Yoga breathing will not change everything. You will still be you, and feel anger, joy, misery and despair, just like you always did. What it can do, however, is give you the power to control your responses to huge events, to rein in powerful emotions and work out what to do with them rather than let them wreak havoc. How many times have you dearly wished that, rather than fly into a rage and shout out what is on your mind, you could wait till you were calm? Or stop and think about the consequences before you get carried along on a wave of excitement? Yoga can give you the power to look before you leap.

### Coping with anger and irritation

The traditional ploy for coping with something that causes anger is to close your eyes and count up to ten. In fact, this is not a half-bad idea, as it gives you a moment to collect yourself. The yoga way is similar. Stand or sit in a comfortable position, keeping your back straight, and close your eyes. Put your hands together, palms facing, in front of you as if you were about to pray and focus on your breathing, taking deeper and slower breaths each time.

As you descend into a more peaceful state you will feel that the edge has been taken off your anger and that you can examine the cause of it in a more level-headed and positive manner.

## Coping with panic and anxiety

Panic usually occurs at a time when you need to act. Unfortunately, panic is the very thing that will prevent you from being able to do so; a state of affairs that will induce even more anxiety! To calm yourself down and get your mental house in order, you need to calm down your heart and breathing. Again, close your eyes and focus on slowing and deepening each breath. If you are sitting at your desk put your hands flat down onto the surface and visualise your panic as an electrical charge that is coursing from your brain, down through your body. Each time you exhale, feel some of that charge exiting through your hands and discharging itself in the work surface. Gradually you will feel calm enough to act.

**NB:** It is essential that you filter out distractions while you do this exercise, and refrain from mentally 'hurrying' yourself up.

## Taking in good or exciting news

Oddly, this can be as stressful as bad news and, once the initial euphoria has worn off, leave you feeling as flat as a pancake and very anticlimactic. To keep yourself in check, put our hands out in front of you, palms downward. Close your eyes and breath slowly. As you exhale, 'push' down with your hands and, as you inhale, allow then to float upwards again.

This exercise will not destroy the pleasure of the experience, merely make your happiness calmer. Thus you will be able to fully take it in, and all its implications.

Ultimately, yoga breathing aims is to treat great emotion with objectivity. Almost as if you were an impartial observer. Even if you never manage this, these exercises will help you to feel that you are in control of them, rather than vice versa.

## Compartmentalisation

Because we lead such busy lives, with so many different demands made of us, many of us feel that our we are living a compartmentalised existence. There is a compartment that is our working life. We change clothes and even personalities, to enter this compartment, becoming harder perhaps, sending out signals of capability and commitment that the inner self may not really feel. Another compartment is home, where we change personalities again, and become more open and loving. This may be the one compartment in which we feel that we are truly being ourselves. There are other compartments, such as the one wherein we meet friends, perhaps more than one group of friends. Little wonder then that we often feel as if our lives are confusing and disconnected, and that there is little room for us to be ourselves.

An interesting way of looking at ourselves is to picture the body as a series of skins, like those of an onion. Sometimes we peel away these skins to reveal our inner selves, while at other times we put them all back on again. It is a way of reconciling all the different aspects of our lives. Consider the outer layer as the outer physical body, the one that most people see and react to. Within this is the inner physical layer, the layer where all the breathing and digestion goes on.

Within that is the conscious mind, where our day to day thinking goes on, where the words that spring out of our physical mouths are generated. Within this is the subconscious, the place where we hoard our memories and work out our feelings, and where our sense of free will comes from. And deep, deep inside this is our inner self, the very core of our being, which is the only part of us that can truly connect with the universe.

Thinking of the body in this way can be a wonderful tool for meditation, and is also a rather soothing thought when you feel as if you are somehow disconnected from yourself. Next time you find yourself in the midst of a busy office, feeling stressed and as if you are putting on an act and wondering how you can be the same person who climbed a mountain at the weekend, or read your children a long, exciting story last night, and did all the actions and felt wonderfully happy, remember that you have simply donned a few more layers this morning and are still the same person inside.

# Chapter 7
# Active Meditation

### Collective meditation

Most non-religious meditations are done on one's own or with a teacher. However, collective or group meditations can also be an extremely positive experience. Group meditation can only work if every group member feels comfortable. In the modern world, where social networks are increasingly becoming the casualties of progress and change, a group of sympathetic minds is something that few people would give up. Most meditation groups stick together for decades.

Groups generally begin a session by picking a topic, perhaps anger management or low self-esteem, and everyone is free to forward their contribution. Group members often remark upon the enormous collective energy they sense at these sessions, where the presence of so many minds focused on one theme engenders heightened creativity. 'It's amazing the insight that people show in these situations,' commented one regular.

Another feature of group meditations, recalling the practices of the Quakers and Carmelites, is the sending of good-will to places across the world that are in trouble. Meditators may hold hands, or simply sit in silence, willing positive energy in the same direction. Participants often feel, at those times, that they are one being, and that their combined mental energy is extremely powerful. Like the Christian lighting a candle, or the Jews gathering to sing praise for the sake of God rather than themselves, this is a means of channelling positive thought at a deserving target. And all enhance the consciousness of the giver.

## The Sufi circle

Most meditations are done on one's own or with a teacher. Movement meditation as practised by some Sufis (best known for their dramatic whirling dancing) is done by groups of five to fifteen people and involves chanting as well.

Form a circle with your companions, standing with feet apart some distance from each other but not so far that you have to stretch your arms as you join hands. Now, very slowly lean backwards raising your face to the ceiling (or sky if you are doing this outdoors) and bring the hands up. When everyone is comfortably looking as straight up as they can, say the words 'Ya Hai' loudly in unison. Now all the people in the group bring their arms down and their heads and bodies forward, until they are facing downwards. Now say in the same ringing, triumphant tone, 'Ya Huk', and return to the 'Ya Hai' position and repeat again and again, establishing a speed and a rhythm comfortable to everyone. Seen from above, the group looks like a blossom opening and closing in perfect harmony.

The point of this meditation is total involvement of awareness of the movement and the accompanying sounds, and each person must be conscious of the physical condition of each of the others in the group. If someone finds that he or she is having to push himself or herself to keep up with the group as it establishes its rhythm, that person steps back and brings the hands of the people on either side together so that the circle remains intact. There must be complete freedom to do this. No one should feel compelled to keep up: if so, the whole point of the meditation is lost.

The aim is to go beyond fatigue to the point where exhaustion is forgotten and all are so lost in the movement and chanting that they become unaware of everything apart from the awareness of self and universe being in total harmony which is the point of all meditation.

Most groups start with ten- to fifteen-minute sessions to establish harmony and a rate at which everyone is comfortable, and when this is achieved, extend the sessions to thirty minutes.

## Sensory awareness meditation

Movement is also a part of this sensory awareness meditation in which it is combined with breathing awareness.

Begin by lying on your back on a rug or mat. Your legs can be fully extended or drawn in towards the buttocks with the feet flat on the floor. When you are comfortable, close your eyes and concentrate for a few minutes on letting each part of the body in turn sink more deeply into the floor, starting with the feet and moving upwards through the calves, knees, thighs, pelvis, rib cage, chest, hands, lower arms, elbows, upper arms and neck to the head. Concentrate not just on the surfaces that are in contact with the floor but with the sides and top too.

Now, concentrating on each exhalation of breath, try to feel your whole body sink deeply into the floor.

After about fifteen minutes, lay the hands on the diaphragm, keeping the upper arms and elbows firmly on the floor. After the diaphragm has moved the hands up and down, up and down for a minute or two, they will feel as if they have been incorporated into the breathing process. Very slowly raise them a little from the body, concentrating all the time on your breathing, then return them to the diaphragm, allowing them once again to become part of the breathing process.

Repeat this for ten minutes or so, gradually increasing the distance the hands are moved away from the body each time until they eventually come to land on the floor. Slowly you will come to think that the whole cycle is happening by itself with absolutely no effort on your part, and you will find yourself at one with the world.

## Tai Chi Ch'uan

Although it is not meditation in the accepted meaning of the word, the aim of Tai Chi (the 'Ch'uan' is usually dropped) is to combine motion, unity and dance so that those who practise its art surrender to the natural flow of the universe and become one with it – exactly the aim of more passive meditation.

Tai Chi is a means of exploring the processes of mind and body through creative movement and reflects the I Ching belief that nature is always in motion. It is said to have originated with the meditation of a Taoist monk, Chang San-feng, who one day saw a magpie trying to attack a snake. The reptile teased the bird by writhing and curling in a spiral motion, always remaining just out of the bird's reach. Similar movements are now an integral part of Tai Chi.

In Tai Chi, the image of water symbolises the flow of energy. It represents the way the flow of energy yields to the form of its container. Earth is seen as a link between person and planet. The use of circular forms of expression shows unity and containment.

It is not possible to learn Tai Chi from the pages of a book. Traditionally the practice was handed down from master to pupil. Today most large towns offer Tai Chi classes, and anyone wishing to learn its ways and mysteries should join a group.

The classes always begin with a period of meditative stillness, and then the pupils step forward on the right foot – an energy step, with fire being visualised shooting from the palms of the hands. Then the energy is pulled back into the body and the weight transferred to the left foot, everyone now visualising water cascading over him or her. With the body turning to the left, the palms are rotated and curved back to the right. The body continues to turn to the right with both feet firmly fixed to the floor, then the left foot is brought round, returning the body to the centre.

Tai Chi is a process of self-discovery and, like yoga, demonstrates the link between body, movement and posture, and contemplative states of being. In the words of one expert, Al Huang, who wrote the classic *Embrace Tiger, Return to Mountain*, 'Tai Chi is to help you get acquainted with your own sense of personal growth, the creative process of just being you.'

Meditation is also traditionally used in other martial arts, including karate and aikido (from the Japanese, *ai* meaning to harmonise, *ki* to control, and *do* meaning way), as a means of marshalling concentration (focus) and maintaining self-discipline, both mentally and physically.

## Attention to life meditation

This is not meditation in the strictest sense of the word, and it is not a method to be used in daily or twice-daily sessions. Rather, it is part of everyday activity, its object being to focus consciously all your attention on the particular movement, activity or task you are performing to the exclusion of everything else.

Take once more something as mundane as dishwashing. As you wash each dish, close your eyes and concentrate on feeling each sensation – the warmth of the water, the texture of the plate, the soapiness of the lather, the smell of the detergent. Focus on each part of the activity. To do so, consciously relax all the muscles not essential to the task and work the muscles actually being used as sparingly as possible.

In focusing your thinking on the task in hand in as concentrated a manner as possible, you are actually meditating, albeit for a very short time, but it is surprising how effective such short-span meditation can be, especially in helping to remove feelings of stress.

## Meditation on the run

Many long-distance runners hit a point, usually about three-quarters of an hour into a run, when they experience what is commonly called a 'high'. This is remarkably similar to what happens during mantra or chanting meditation, with the rhythmic repetition of the word or phrase being replaced by the rhythm of the run. The runner's conscious mind shuts down, allowing other areas of consciousness to open up.

So, if you enjoy a jog, use it not just to make the body fit, but to put your mind in better shape too.

Don't try to compete with other runners in the park or against the clock to beat your own personal best time. If you do, you are shutting your mind to the possibility of meditation. Run easily, establishing a regular rhythm, and focus your attention on your breathing, your pulse and heartbeat, and after a while you will reach a point where you will be as perfectly in tune with the world as a Buddhist monk sitting hour after hour in contemplative meditation

# Chapter 8

# Mantras

Repeating a word or phrase – a mantra – over and over again is probably the most practised and widespread path to meditation and one of the oldest. Mantra yoga is mentioned in the Vedas, the oldest of the world's scriptures. The mantra may be chanted aloud or repeated silently. The repetition of the mantra is known in India as japa, and according to the traditions of that country there are fourteen different kinds of japa. Today, in the West, only two of them are in common use – voiced repetition and mental repetition.

The power of the mantra is the power of sound to affect people and alter their state of mind. If you doubt that sound can do this, pause for a moment and consider how irritated you get if someone is playing music too loudly or if you are sitting next to someone who is plugged into a personal stereo and the music is almost audible to you. If sound can irritate, then surely the converse is true – sound can make you feel tranquil, and to focus on a mantra during meditation can lead to some of the deepest and most profound sessions you are likely to experience.

Sound is energy produced by a vibrating object. We can hear waves within a certain frequency band, and we interpret different frequencies as different sounds. If the frequencies are above this band, they are called ultrasonic, if below, infrasonic. The body absorbs all frequencies, even the ones that the ear cannot hear, and they can have a profound effect upon us, even to the extent of altering our moods. This influence is now being utilised in some forms of therapy.

There is also the matter of resonance. This latter is the phenomena whereby one vibration can cause another, as, for example, someone singing a clear, high, sustained note might produce a ringing resonance in a crystal glass. Mantras are not arbitrary gatherings of words that sound pleasant, but deliberate constructions that utilise the phenomena of sound, frequency and resonance. Followers of mantra meditation believe that the mantra sounds resonate with different energy centres in the body.

Most of the major religions have their own mantra, and a selection of these are described at the end of this section. For those who wish to use a mantra in their meditation but who want to avoid religion, any word or phrase, no matter how meaningless, will do.

In India, until the eleventh century, it was usual for gurus to devise personal mantras for each of their pupils. Each pupil treasured his mantra and refused to divulge it to his fellows for he had been warned that in doing so the power of the mantra would be weakened. In the eleventh century, Ramanuja, a leading figure in the history of Indian yoga and one suspicious of the almost mystical power of the gurus, shouted his mantra from the roof of a temple so that all could share it. The practice of secret mantras now only survives, generally speaking, in the school of Transcendental Meditation (TM) practised by the Maharishi Mahesh.

Those who are suspicious of any religious aspects associated with mantra can do little better than choose their mantra by the method recommended by a Lawrence LeShant, a leading expert in the subject. He advocates the 'La-de' method of mantra selection: simply opening a telephone directory at random and blindly letting the forefinger fall on the page. The first syllable of that name becomes the first syllable of the mantra. Repeat the process, linking the second syllable selected at random with the first and – hey presto! – you have a mantra.

To practise meditation with a mantra, begin, as usual, by taking up the position that you find most comfortable and breathe gently and rhythmically through the nostrils, taking the breath deep into the abdomen. Then repeat the mantra, either aloud or silently inward, focusing your concentration on it as completely as you can. When your mind has become still, it is no longer necessary to continue repeating the mantra, but, as with other forms of meditation, when you become aware that your thoughts have wandered, start repeating the mantra again, concentrating your conscious thoughts on it.

Once you have chosen a mantra with which you are comfortable, stick with it. It's amazing how in times of stress, repeating your mantra a few times silently to yourself restores calm and helps you to put things into proper perspective.

Many mantra meditators repeat the mantra in rhythm with their breathing, saying it once or twice on inhalation and once or twice on breathing out. They are usually repeated silently, but some teachers encourage their pupils to say them aloud, especially if they are leading a group meditation.

## Om

Om, a Sanskrit word pronounced to rhyme with 'Rome', is one of the most widely used mantras. According to Hindu belief, om is the primal sound and it is accorded the highest value as an object of meditation and one well worth trying. Breathe in gently, and as you exhale recite the word as three sounds, 'a' (as in father), 'oo' (as in room) and 'mmm'. Try to feel the sounds vibrating in your body. The 'a' will feel as if it is ringing in your belly, the 'oo' will resonate in your chest and the 'mmm' will positively resound in the bones of your skull. Link the sounds to your breathing rhythm, keeping it slow and calm and avoiding deepening it in any way.

After saying om aloud for ten breaths, soften the voice until you are saying the word under your breath, then lower it even further, keeping your attention firmly focused on it. It won't be long before your lips stop moving and the syllables lose their shape, leaving you with just an idea that clings to your mind. Banish any intrusive thoughts by imagining them as puffs of smoke and watch them being blown away by a gentle breeze.

## The Jesus prayer

Some Christians use the name of Jesus as their mantra, others use short prayers, one of the most popular of which is the Jesus prayer which was probably devised by Orthodox monks. It has two forms, either 'Lord Jesus Christ, son of God, have mercy on me', or 'Lord Jesus Christ, have mercy on me'. The prayer is not meant as a petition but follows the advice of a seventh-century mystic who is reputed to have written, 'If many words are used in prayer, all sorts of distracting pictures hover in the mind, but worship is lost. If little is said . . . the mind remains concentrated.' His words could be paraphrased to define mantra – a few words to concentrate the mind.

## The rosary

You do not have to be Roman Catholic to meditate on the rosary; any Christian can use the beads as a focus for their meditation. With your eyes closed, pass the beads slowly through the fingers, noticing how the smaller beads are periodically punctuated by large ones. Each time you finger a small bead repeat the words of the Hail Mary:

> Hail Mary, full of grace,
> The Lord is with thee.
> Blessed art thou among women
> And blessed is the fruit of thy womb, Jesus.
> Hail Mary, Mother of God,
> Pray for us sinners now
> And at the hour of our death.
> Amen

Move on to the next bead: if it is small, repeat the Hail Mary, if it is one of the larger beads, say the Lord's Prayer. The meditation should last for the usual twenty minutes.

## Humming like a bee

While not exactly a mantra in the true sense of the word, there are many people who hum while meditating. If you would like to try this, take up your usual position but close your right nostril with your right thumb and inhale through the left nostril, holding your breath as deep and as low in the abdomen as you can. Now exhale and as you do so make a humming noise deep in your throat, focusing your thoughts on the sound.

Do this five times and repeat the exercise with the right nostril, then alternate five times with each nostril for the full twenty-minute meditation.

## Transcendental meditation

This form of mantra meditation was introduced to the West in 1959 by the Maharishi Mahesh. It became popular in the 1960s when several influential young men and women, pop stars prominent amongst them, claiming they were disillusioned with Western values, turned to the East for spiritual fulfilment. Its central feature is contemplation on and repetition of a Sanskrit mantra personally bestowed on each follower by his or her guru, originally Mahesh himself.

In the Maharishi's own words, in TM '. . . the attention comes from outside to the inside, to the source of thought, and then the conscious mind . . . gains that transcendent pure awareness which is bliss consciousness. It is just thinking, but thinking in a manner so that awareness goes deep within and gains that inner being of pure consciousness.'

Those who follow TM meditate for forty minutes a day in two periods of twenty minutes, repeating their mantra inwardly without moving the lips. The two periods of meditation must be separated by at least six hours of normal activity. Unlike many other Indian schools of meditation, TM demands no conscious changes in lifestyle. The Maharishi claims that such changes will happen spontaneously as the meditation sessions progress.

A great deal of research was conducted on TM, and it emerged that it did create significant psychological changes associated with relaxation. Sceptics, however, queried the methodology of much of the research, and their constant barracking weakened the validity of some of the findings. Those who follow TM insist on the mantra being chosen with much ceremony and in secrecy by the master teacher, but this practice has not been shown to be any more effective than one that uses simple words.

TM is perhaps most renowned for the seemingly bizarre practise of yogic flying, which is said to produce feelings of 'bubbling bliss for the individual, reducing stress and enlivening positivity in the environment.'

**Who says what:**

*Buddhism*
Buddhist mantras are associated with mandalas (*see* page 131) – images of the cosmos, prayer wheels and beads and counters. It is common among Buddhists to repeat the mantra 108 times because of the significance of the numbers: 1 is the absolute; 0 is the cosmos; and 8 is the infinite.

| | |
|---|---|
| Gate, Gate, Pargate, Paramsagate, Svahag | Gone, gone, gone to the other shore, safely passed to Bodhi that other shore, Enlightened One |
| Namo Buddya, Namo Dharmaya, Namo Sanghaya | I go to the Buddha for refuge, I go to the Dharma for refuge, I go to the Sangha for refuge |
| Bhagavan Sarva Tathagatha Tathagatha | Blessed be all your Buddhas |

| | |
|---|---|
| Om Tare Tutare Ture Swaha | Hail to Tara |
| Namo Amitabha | I go to the Buddha for light |
| Om Mani Padme Hum | Hail to the Jewel in the Lotus |

*Sikhism*

| | |
|---|---|
| Eck Ong Kar Sat Nam Siri Wha Guru | The Supreme is one, His names are many |

*Hinduism*

| | |
|---|---|
| Tat Tuam Asi | Thou art that |
| So ham | That I am |
| Hare Krishna | Hail to Krishna |
| Hare Rama | Hail to Rama |
| Om Namah Sivaya, Shanti, Shanti | Om reverence to Shiva, peace, peace |

The following mantras have particular healing associations for Hindus:

| | |
|---|---|
| Hrim | (throat and liver) |
| Hrum | (liver and spleen) |
| Hraim | (kidneys) |
| Hra | (heart and chest) |

*Islam*

| | |
|---|---|
| Allah, Allah, La Ilaha Illa'llah | God, God, there is no God but one God |

| | |
|---|---|
| Insha Allah | If God wills |
| Ya-Salaam | God, the source of peace |
| An-Nur | God, the light |

*Judaism*

| | |
|---|---|
| Adonai | Lord |
| Shalom | Peace |
| Ehyeh Asher Ehyeh | I am that I am |
| Quadosh, Quadosh, Quadosh Adonai Tzeba'oth | Holy, Holy, Holy Lord of Hosts |
| Eli, Eli, Eli Barukh Ata Adonai | My God, My God, My God Blessed is the Lord |

*Christianity*

| | |
|---|---|
| Lord Jesus Christ, Son of God, Have Mercy on us | |
| Kyrie Eleison, Christe Eleison, Kyrie Eleison | Lord have mercy, Christ have mercy, God have mercy |
| Laudamus | We praise thee |
| Alleluia | |
| Holy, Holy, Holy | |
| En Emoi Christus | Christ in me |

| Ave Maria | Hail Mary |
| --- | --- |

*Sufism*

| Hu-E-Haiy | God the living |
| --- | --- |
| He-La | The word is the mirror wherein the Divine reverberates outwardly. |
| | Through sound the world will be reabsorbed. The word is both sound and light, for light is the meaning of the word |

# Chapter 9

# Visual Meditation

Visual meditation uses our natural capacity to think in pictures and our ability to create images in what is often called the mind's eye. It may be practised with the eyes open or shut or by opening and shutting them for alternate periods, concentrating on the afterimage that remains in our mind when the eyes are closed. The latter method is most usually recommended for beginners.

### Tratek (gazing meditation)

Gazing meditation involves contemplating an object without judgement or thought, simply revelling in its existence. Choose your object with care: you want something neither too complex nor with negative associations for you. If thoughts intrude upon your meditation, chase them away by renewing your attentions on your chosen object.

Place the object of your meditation (on which more later) at eye level between a metre and two metres from your face. If you decide to use a mandala or yantra (*see* pages 131–134) the central point should be level with the eyes. Assume whichever meditation position you favour, and in as relaxed a way as possible, gaze at the image, focusing your attention on it, trying to become absorbed in what you are looking at rather than just thinking about it.

After two or three minutes or as soon as you feel any indication of eye strain, close your eyes and visualise the object for as long as you can, still attempting to be part of it. Open your eyes again and continue alternating open-eyed and closed-eyed meditation for the full session.

Initially it will be difficult to retain the image in your mind's eye for long when your eyes are closed: don't worry. When the image starts to fade, open the eyes and gaze at the object again. As you become more practised in the art, you will find that you can retain the image for longer and longer.

## Meditating on a candle

Many of those who come to visual meditation for the first time find that a lighted candle in a darkened room is the ideal object of focus. This may be because we associate a candle flame with peace and enlightenment, and find it both a comforting and inspiring thing to gaze upon.

One method recommended for beginners is to light a candle in a darkened, draught-free room: draught-free so that the flame burns as steadily as possible. To meditate on a candle, sit as motionless as you can in any of the recommended positions and gaze at the flame so that it holds your attention completely. Do not analyse why this image fascinates you, or allow your mind to wander onto thoughts of the candle's heat or brightness: simply look. Let the image fill your mind for a minute before quickly closing the eyes. Notice how the candle has imprinted itself on the darkness. Hold it in your mind's eye, not worrying about any change of colour. If it slips to the side, bring it back to the centre and keep concentrating until the image fades completely. Now open the eyes and resume gazing at the candle. Continue in this way for ten minutes at first, gradually increasing the time until you can sit comfortably for a full twenty-minutes.

## A flower or a bowl

Some people begin their visualising techniques with a flower. One expert tells his novice pupils to gaze at a patterned china bowl, taking it all in at first, then allowing the eyes to travel over it, tracing its lines and colours, the pattern that decorates it, the way it catches the light. Only when his pupils come to experience the bowl's visual qualities for the first time, does he move on to telling them to close their eyes and try to focus on the image of the bowl held in the mind.

## It takes practice

At first, it is hard to hold a mental picture of the object, but with practice it becomes easier and easier until the point is reached when the actual object can be abandoned completely and you can meditate on the mental image with no external visual stimulus being used. This can be extremely difficult, and if you have been successful with the alternating method but have had problems when you have tried to meditate holding a mental image in your mind for the entire session, you have probably been trying too hard or expecting too much. It can take years of practice before you can see the image clearly. Think of the mind as a musical instrument that has to be tuned with patience and sensitivity before it can be used to produce beautiful music.

Some who practise visual meditation find it helps to train the mind by closing the eyes and picturing a friend, concentrating on each feature in turn, the colour of the skin and hair, the shape and colour of the eyes, and so on, and then returning to the complete face, holding on to the image for as long as they can, and when it starts to blur, focusing again on the separate features.

## Many different symbols

Roman Catholics and Anglicans have long used the image of Christ on the cross as a symbol in visualisation meditation. Christians who belong to the 'low' Churches often meditate on the empty cross, while many people who belong to the Orthodox Church use small painted panels bearing an image of Christ or the Virgin Mary or any of the saints as visualisation symbols.

Buddhists may meditate on a mental image of Buddha himself or one of the other Buddhas, especially Tara, the liberator, the mother of all Buddhas. They see her as the manifestation of all that is positive. Bathed in radiant emerald-green light, swathed in silk and bedecked with jewels, she smiles lovingly at those who focus their meditations on her.

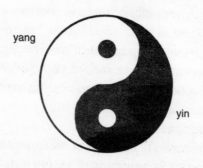

*The Chinese yin and yang symbol*

Jewish meditators might visualise the Tree of Life that represents the Sefirot, or ten divine energies, or the characters of the Hebrew alphabet.

Chinese meditators often use the famous Yin-yang symbol. This symbol represents the perfect whole of nature, created by the balance of two counterforces. Yin without yang is like north without south or rain without sunshine. One is dark and feminine, the other bright and masculine, and meditating upon this balance of life engenders a sense of oneness with the environment.

The *Visuddhimagga*, a fourth-century Buddhist text, lists ten different subjects for visual meditation. These are known as kasinas and comprise air, earth, fire and water (the four elements), blue, yellow, red and green (the four colours of nature), light and space. To meditate on any of the elements, the meditator simply stares at an appropriate object, a pot filled with earth, for example, or a bowl of water. To visualise any of the four colours, simply gaze at an object of that colour – a flower, a piece of fabric, anything at all. To meditate on light, focus the attention on the light cast by a light bulb, and any empty container can be used as a focus when meditating on space.

Buddhists, in common with Hindus, also use mandalas, the most famous of which is probably the Buddhist wheel of life, and Hindus commonly meditate on yantras (*see* below).

**Yantras and mandalas**

To scholars of Sanskrit, yantra is a word meaning 'instrument', and mandala is a word that means 'circle' – the supreme universal symbol. To the meditator, a yantra is a diagram that possesses the power to transform the consciousness of those who have been introduced to knowledge of what the yantras represent.

A mandala is essentially a type of yantra, the yantra being more specific to a particular deity, the mandala being more general. Both are diagrammatic in form, designed so that the focus of the meditator comes to rest on a central focal point, the bindu, which is said to represent the essence of being.

They can be astonishingly beautiful, especially those of Tibetan Tantric Buddhists whose richly symbolic and intricately designed mandalas have come to be prise d by collectors as fine works of art.

There is another aspect of Tantric Buddhism that Westerners find fascinating, mistaking it more often than not as an indulgence of the sexual appetites rather than a tool for medi-

*An example of a mandala*

tation – maithuna, or ritual sexual intercourse. Those who practise it claim that it is a potent means of allowing kundalini energy – the force awakened by meditation on the chakras (*see* page 253) – to be released, allowing the yogi to move on to meditating a higher chakra. Before performing maithuna, the yogi performs certain rituals and recites the mantra given to him by his guru as well as other mantras that are part of the rituals. Maithuna must be carried out in the prescribed manner, the yogi having been taught exactly where and how he may touch his partner's body. It is the female who is active during maithuna, since its aim is in the arousal of energy rather than in the climax, at which moment the yogi consecrates his semen as a sacrificial offering.

The lotus blossom, the symbol of enlightenment, is widely used as part of the patterns, symbolising the unfolding of creation. According to Hindu mythology, Brahma stood at the centre of a thousand-petalled lotus before creating the universe, and Buddhists believe that at the birth of the Buddha, a large lotus sprang from the earth, and Buddha stepped into its centre. From there he gazed into the ten directions of space, once along each of the eight petals, once upwards and once downwards.

Mandalas and yantras may be drawn, painted or carved in stone. Some eastern mystics even meditate on yantras that they draw for themselves in the sand or earth. Such temporary ones often serve as teaching aids between master and pupils.

## Meditating with a mandala or yantra
Before you can meditate with a mandala or yantra you will

have to be instructed on its meaning. Then, place it so that the central point is at eye level when you are sitting before it in your usual meditating position. Relax the muscles of your face and sit absolutely motionless, gazing at the centre point. Let your gaze move slowly outwards to the edge, taking in but trying not to think about the visual content. Now let the gaze move slowly back to the centre before closing the eyes and holding the image in your mind's eye for as long as you can before opening the eyes again and repeating the process. As you become more practised, you will find that your eye will automatically be drawn to the centre and that it rests there effortlessly on the point that symbolise s the essence of being.

## The space between the eyebrows meditation

This space corresponds to the ajna chakra (*see* page 251). Sit, kneel or lie in your usual position with your eyes closed. Gently swivel your eyeballs upwards and try to visualise them as focused on the space between your eyebrows. See how close this space is to the brain – feel its central position, visualise viewing it from the outside: now visualise it from the inside. The space between the eyebrows is a part of you. As the meditation deepens feel yourself becoming a part of that space. If unwanted thoughts intrude, mentally blow them away and return your focus to the space between the eyebrows.

## Colour visualising

There are many methods of using colour as a means of reaching the meditative state. The two given here are among the simplest.

For the first, sit in whichever position you favour and begin to breathe deeply. As usual, don't force the breath, but let it find its own pace and depth. When it has settled to a slow, rhythmic rate, begin to visualise the colours red, orange and yellow, flowing upwards into your solar plexus, visualising each colour one at a time as a gently flowing river.

Spend a minute or so on each colour and then picture a stream of green flowing into the solar plexus from directly in front of you. After a minute or so, follow the green with blue, indigo and violet, each in turn flowing into you from the same source as the green.

Once the spectrum is completed, imagine yourself bathed in a blue light before ending the meditation by opening your eyes.

Do not be put off if at first you find it rather difficult to visualise a colour: with practice this becomes easier.

The second method is to sit with eyes closed before focusing the thoughts on any colour you wish. Fill your mind with that colour to the exclusion of everything else and refuse to be frustrated by other thoughts that may come to mind.

Wrap them slowly in the colour so that they are enveloped in it. It sometimes helps to imagine an object of your chosen shade – a field of yellow corn perhaps – and gradually concentrate your thoughts on it until the field becomes totally unimportant and your mind is a canvas of yellow.

Some people who practise colour meditation, in fact, begin each session by picturing an easel on which rests a blank canvas that stroke by stroke fills up with the chosen colour.

## Body of light visualising

This is an advanced meditation. Sit comfortably with your back straight, breathing naturally. When your mind is clear and calm, visualise the space above your head as a sphere of white light slightly smaller in size than your head. Try to see it as pure and transparent, and spend several minutes concentrating on it.

See the sphere of light as representing goodness, wisdom and love – as the fulfilment of your own highest potential. Then visualise that it is getting smaller and smaller until it is about two centimetres in diameter and that slowly it begins to descend through your head towards your heart, then begins to expand once more until it spreads to every part of your body. As it does so, see it dissolve all the organs and solid parts of your body until they too become pure, formless white light.

Concentrate on the perception of your body as a mass of light and believe all your problems, negative emotions and the things that hold you back have disappeared. Let any thoughts or distractions dissolve in the light, and with practice you will achieve a joyful serenity and reach a state of wholeness and perfection.

## Purification visualising

Purification is a recurring theme in Buddhist meditation. When we see ourselves as impure or negative, that is what we become. With our self-esteem at a low ebb we feel limited and inadequate and don't give ourselves a chance to change. Believing that we are pure in essence is the first step to becoming pure in practice.

This simple meditation contains the essence of purification, banishing problems and mistakes, trying to see them as temporary intrusions, not as part of our nature.

Begin by settling comfortably into a suitable position, then concentrate on breathing normally and observing how long each exhalation and inhalation lasts. After a minute or two, imagine that all your negative energy, the mistakes you have made in the past, the things that are holding you back are leaving your body in a cloud of black smoke each time you breathe out. When you inhale, visualise that everything positive in the universe is entering your body in a stream of white light, as radiant as it is pure. Visualise it flowing to every part of your body, bathing it in its intensity.

Banish distractions by seeing them as black smoke and exhale them along with the other negative aspects of your experience.

## Bubbles of thought meditation

Sitting in a comfortable position, visualise your mind as the smooth, calm surface of a pond. As thoughts enter your mind, see them as bubbles rising from the depths of the pond. They should be observed, not pursued, so that the conscious and deliberate following through of each thought is avoided and you become detached from it as you watch it bubble to the surface. Note the thought and then gently return to contemplating the smooth, rippleless surface of the pond.

As time passes and you pass into deeper layers of consciousness, see yourself sinking under the surface of the pond, becoming one with it.

After about ten minutes, refocus your mind on your surroundings to bring the meditation to a conclusion.

## A visual stress buster

Think of a scene that has meant a lot to you, such as a beautiful sunrise on the last morning of a glorious holiday, or a pebbly beach that you used to visit as a child. Your memory may not be exact, but try to conjure up in your mind's eye the colours of the sky, the sounds, the smells. Think of this as a place that is lodged deep inside you, a place that you take with you everywhere.

When the phone rings off the wall, unpaid bills are mounting up, the boss wants to talk to you about your future with the company, and the children are fighting, take ten minutes for yourself. Sit down in the posture you prefer, close your eyes, focus on your breathing, and let it take you inside yourself to that peaceful beautiful place. It may sound corny, but memories wield a powerful influence over our emotions and wellbeing, and the memory of calm and happiness, if recalled sufficiently deeply, can induce similar feelings in the present.

## Visual meditation and health

Although the following is not meditation in the true sense of the word, visualisation is required, and we demonstrate how it can be used to treat two specific health problems. Space precludes us from dealing with more ailments and how they may be treated, but if you try the ones discussed below, perhaps you may be tempted to look further into this area: it can be extremely rewarding.

Assume your usual meditation posture unless your malady prevents it, in which case, make yourself as comfortable as you can with the back as straight as you can get it and the head in perfect alignment. Concentrate on your breathing for a moment or two until it becomes settled and regular.

For painful joints, picture the affected area in your mind and visualise the blood vessels leading to and from it congested with dark red blood. Notice how taut the muscles are and how tangled the nerves. With this image firmly fixed, see a tide of pink, oxygen-full blood, enriched with healing white cells, flood through the veins and arteries. Observe how the muscles relax and your nerves untangle. Hold this image in your mind and then visualise the whole area again free from congestion, the muscles working smoothly, the nerves strands of polished wire. Let the image fade from view and, hopefully, the pain will have eased.

For bronchial problems, visualise your lungs clogged with dark yellow mucus. Now see the colour lighten, starting from the bottom of each lung until the mucous membranes are producing just enough mucus to keep the lungs properly lubricated and there is a ball of mucus being pushed up your throat and coughed out. You should be breathing much more easily at the end of this visualisation.

Similar techniques, where the affected area is visualised first in its stricken state then as being cleansed before being seen in perfect working order, can be applied to a whole host of complaints. When all else fails, why not try them?

# Chapter 10

# Advanced Meditation Techniques

### Inner heat meditation

This is an extremely advanced meditation requiring sophisticated breathing techniques as well as visualisation. It is included here as an example of the most demanding meditation techniques. It was developed by a Tibetan Buddhist who believed that mental energy flows through the body within an invisible psychic nervous system made up of thousands of thin, transparent channels. The principal ones – the central, right and left channels – run parallel to and just in front of the spinal column. Pure mental energy can function within the central channel whereas diluted (deluded) energy flows through the others.

In our normal state, the central channel is blocked by knots of nervous energy at the various chakras (*see* page 245). This energy blocks pure energy from the mind, making it unable to function properly.

Inner heat meditation is an excellent method for transforming powerful negative energy, helping us to develop spontaneous control over all actions of body, speech and mind.

Begin by adopting your usual meditation posture, settle your thoughts and your breathing, and visualise the central channel as a transparent, hollow tube, about the same diameter as your forefinger, running straight down the centre of the body just in front of the spinal column, from the crown of your head to the base of your spine.

Now visualise the left and right channels, slightly thinner than the central one, starting from the left and right nostril respectively, reaching up to the top of the head then curving to run downwards on either side of the central channel before curving inwards to join the central channel about a hand's-breadth below the navel.

Take your time. There is no hurry whatsoever, and once the visualisation (some people say it helps to see it as a very simple central heating system) is firmly fixed, imagine a red-hot ember the size of a seed inside the central channel level with the navel. If it helps to strengthen this visualisation, see yourself reaching into a fire and taking out a small ember that you put in place.

When you really feel the intense heat, gently contract the lower pelvic muscles and see air energy rising from the lowest chakra up to the ember. Now breathe deeply through both nostrils, seeing the air travelling down the left and right channels round into the central channel, where it joins with the heat and air energy brought up from below.

When you have inhaled, swallow and push down gently with the diaphragm, compressing the energy brought down from above: the air energy is locked in, trapped from above and below.

Now hold the breath as long as possible without forcing it and concentrate on the glowing ember in the navel area, its heat now spreading through the compressed air energy.

When you breathe out, visualise the warm air rising through

the central channel, seeing it burn away the negative energies that are blocking each of the chakras.

Repeat the cycle seven times, intensifying the heat with each breath. By the time you breathe out for the seventh time, visualise the ember bursting into flames, shooting up the central channel and burning out the remaining negative energy in the chakras. When the flames reach the crown of the head, they melt into wonderful, almost sensual, energy that rushes down the now pure central channel, intensifying in pleasure as it passes each chakra, finally engulfing the remains of the ember and making it explode in a blissful heat that reaches every cell of your body, filling you with happiness.

If you ever succeed in this meditation, don't try to analyse the bliss, just accept it, relax, enjoy and concentrate on it calmly and in a controlled manner. It is, as we said, extremely complex, but those who have mastered it believe it is, the best of all visual meditation techniques.

To an extent you have developed self-mastery. This may be as far as you wish to go. In time, however, you may wish to take this process of self-mastery a stage further through the practise of Raja yoga, the king of all yogas. Raja yoga helps to still the vrittis, which are the thought waves, allowing you to know your true self.

Think of the mind as a lake and the vrittis as ripples. Every stray thought causes a ripple, making it harder to see down through the water at your real self. The objective is to still the mind till it is like the surface of a smooth, mirror-like lake. Meditation is the yoga way of achieving this inner stillness. There are three stages, pratyahara, dharana and dhyana, to be completed before the self-realisation can be achieved, though it is entirely up to the individual how far along this path they wish to go, and at what speed.

## Withdrawal of senses (pratyahara)

The fifth limb of yoga is pratyahara, which means 'gathering inwards'. It involves the withdrawal of senses, or, to put it in more straightforward terms, releasing the mind from its domination by the senses. This does not mean numbing the senses so that our taste, sight, hearing, sense of touch and smell are so impaired that we cannot enjoy the outside world! Rather it means controlling our reactions to sense impressions. The value of this can be seen immediately if you consider the sense impressions we receive from a headache; being able to distance ourselves from that misery would be a wonderful thing indeed. However, it also has value in connection with everyday sense impressions as it enables us to fully tune into our mind and analyse its workings.

In fact, we control our senses on a regular basis without actually realising it. Sprinters, for example, sometimes talk about the 'white tunnel' they seem to run through when their mind's energy is totally locked into winning the race. The sounds of the crowd, even the presence of the other runners, is screened out so that they can concentrate. On a more mundane level, think of reading an enthralling novel and suddenly looking up to find that the daylight has faded, the fire has gone out, and you have been feeling cold without even noticing.

Our sense organs are not infallible, and can easily be 'tricked'. A hypnotist, for example, can convince a person to eat an onion and enjoy it as if were a lovely juicy apple. While this is done in the cause of entertainment, hypnosis can be used to achieve positive ends, such as giving up smoking. In this case, the hypnotist persuades the patient's senses to loathe the smell and taste of the habit they previously felt that they enjoyed, and plants in the mind the belief that smoking is no longer needed as an emotional prop. However, the effects of such hypnosis do not always last and the reason for this is that the anti-smoking impetus has been planted in the mind by someone else. An idea created from within is much stronger, because you are the one in control, and the one who can reinforce it.

Faith healing works in much the same way, and is more powerful because it prompts the person being 'healed' to take control. The healer has no 'magic touch', but by convincing them that he has, their mind believes the body to be healed and responds to sense impressions differently and becomes less overwhelmed by them. The result is often a 'miraculous' reduction in pain and discomfort.

Controlling our senses the yoga way requires no such external intervention, but it does require a lot of practice. The Bhagavad Gita recommends an almost scientific approach of practising the observation of your sense impressions almost as if they did not belong to you. The Scottish poet Iain Crichton Smith, when he suffered a long illness, feared that he would never again hear the 'inner handle' of his mind. The 'inner handle' to which he referred was that part of himself, deep inside, that could distance itself from his senses and emotions in order to observe them and capture their essence in poetry. His illness barred his way by dominating him with miserable and insistent sense impressions.

An exercise that can help you to tap into this inner self is to sit very quietly and sink into the experience of simply sitting. Close your eyes and be alert to every sound and smell, the distant roar of traffic, the hum of a lawnmower, the scent of the air coming through the window. Now think of yourself hearing and smelling these things, think of how the sounds are not a part of you but threads of information that your ear transmits to your brain. Think of the inner you that receives these threads of information, and rather than interpret the messages, deciding whether you like them or not, or letting your mind drift off on thoughts and memories triggered by them, just home in on that inner self.

On a practical note, try this exercise the next time you have a headache. Think of the pain and what part of your head is sending this message to your brain. Again, think of it as a thread of information, like a radio wave, that your inner self is receiving. Home in on that inner self and you will find that the pain recedes from the front of your consciousness.

With practise you will eventually be able to tap into the gaps between thoughts, moments of utter tranquillity to which we very rarely get access. This is pratyahara, the first stage of turning inwards and the first step towards self-realisation, which is called samadhi.

## Concentration (dharana) and contemplation (dhyana)

The sixth limb of yoga is concentration; the art of focusing on a single idea or object. This sounds simple enough, but in fact we rarely achieve it. Consider how often you forget what you were about to say, or lose track of a train of thought. This happens because the mind tends to flit from one thought to the other, especially when we become adults and have so much more to think about. Children, by comparison, are often to be seen utterly absorbed in a project, say a painting or even simply staring out the window at the shapes of clouds. Adults tend to be wary about throwing themselves into a task in case there is something more important that they should be thinking about. Women are especially prone to this, particularly if they have young children, as they develop almost an extra sense that is forever on the alert for signals of their offspring's distress. The drawback of all this mental activity is that it can be irritating being unable to concentrate, and therefore stressful, and can also hamper our chances of success in life.

We refer to successful people as 'single-minded' and 'focused', meaning that they know what they want and concentrate on getting it. This sometimes carries with it the negative connotation of meaning that the person is overambitious, even ruthless, and has little time or thought for anything other than their personal success. Single-minded people, according to popular perception, stay in the office till all hours, take work home, and ignore their families. But in fact, being focused need not be negative at all. Sportspeople, performers and artists all need to be able to focus in order to achieve. A distracted artist would never complete any paintings, a distracted athlete fail to win a single race. Concentration is the key to mental and physical success.

It is also the key to revelation. Mystics have claimed to see great and wonderful visions through intense prayer or meditation. On a secular level, it is believed that the great thinkers and inventors of past ages came upon their discoveries through meditation upon a single object or idea, projecting the power of the whole mind in one direction. It is often said that the hardest part of invention is working out what to invent; the hows and whys are quite straightforward by comparison. Consider how James Watt came to discover the power of steam. From gazing at the steam coming out of a kettle, he came to realise that here was a source of energy that could be exploited for the benefit of mankind. Had he been staring at it but thinking about what to have for dinner, or what the weather was likely to be like tomorrow, the great age of steam may have been severely delayed.

Concentration can also lead to personal fulfilment, if only because it makes us more productive and thereby allows us more time away from the workplace. It also enables us to pay attention to, and prioritise, the different segments of our lives. Many people with busy careers find that they waste their leisure time worrying about work, resulting in a failure to give family and personal affairs their due attention. Dharana helps us to plug our thoughts back into every area of our lives. This is called samprajanya, which means awareness of all things.

## Practising dharana and dhyana

To practice dharana, ensure first of all that you are sitting comfortably, in the thunderbolt or half-lotus for instance. If you are uncomfortable your mind will constantly be distracted by negative signals, and the exercise will become pointless. Take a few minutes to relax, breathing deeply from your diaphragm. Concentrating on your breathing will assist in the process of clearing your mind. Now find a small object to concentrate upon. A giant hillside or full-size painting will have your eyes, and mind, darting all over the place! Select something like a pretty stone, a flower, or a small photograph, something which you like and will make you feel positive. You might want to keep certain objects aside specifically for this purpose, perhaps a piece of sea-softened glass that you found on a beautiful beach or a small sculpture made by a child. The object does not need to have religious or talismanic significance; it is simply a tool for aiding concentration.

A good beginner's exercise is to take the object of your choice, let us say it is a seashell, and imagine how you would paint it. Examine the colours, the way that certain hues repeat themselves in patterns, and how the texture varies from smooth to rough. Now close your eyes and run your fingers round and inside the shell, feeling the textures. Bring it close to your nose and inhale the scent. Think of where it came from, how it was washed ashore by the sea and how the waves softened it over time. Think of the creature that once inhabited it. As you do this exercise you will come to appreciate the essence of the shell itself, and be able to summon it up almost as a single thought. The shell will become a fusion of its colours, textures, smell and history. Learning to focus on the essence of an object or idea is called dhyana, which means contemplation.

A good way to build up your concentration skills throughout the day is to try a little Zen living. Pour yourself a glass of water. Allow the tap to run till the water is very cold, and listen to the sound of the water as it fills the glass, and feel its coldness seeping through to your hand. As you drink, think about the feel of it in your mouth, the sensation of refreshing coolness as you swallow. Think of how this pure substance is acting to purify your system, helping your kidneys to flush out toxins and helping to keep your body hydrated. By the time you have finished, your mind will feel as refreshed as your body.

Eventually you will learn to spot focus on an object. To do this, locate the central spot of the object and focus your gaze there rather than allow it to wander around. Imagine your sight as two lines that converge at this spot and keep that point of convergence steady. Allow your facial muscles and shoulders to relax; screwing up your eyes will only make you tense. Try not to be frustrated by the fact that, inevitably, your first attempts will be hindered by your thoughts' tendency to waver off course. Do not be discouraged, or even the least bit surprised, if your mind starts working out next month's disposable income or making a mental 'things to do' list for the weekend. Simply acknowledge the fact that you have wandered and steer your mind back. Don't stop to analyse these thoughts and where they came from, simply push them away. Some people find that a physical gesture, such as batting the thoughts away like flies, can help.

You will gradually become better and better at batting away stray thoughts, and your mental straying will begin to diminish. Initially it requires effort, but it will become effortless.

*Visualisation*
Practising dharana with your eyes shut helps to control the senses and can thus make focusing easier. Most of us are naturally very good at visualisation and can close our eyes and summon up images in our mind's eye at will. We do it when we daydream and when we dream in our sleep. Honing your visualisation skills will not only benefit your ability to meditate, it will also enhance your life, enabling you to store up 'snapshots' that make you happy or inspire you, to be recalled whenever you want them.

*A visualisation journey*

This requires you to lie on your back in the corpse posture. Make sure that you are not too cold or warm and that your body feels comfortable as this will take some time. Take a series of deep breaths and let yourself be heavy into the floor. As you exhale, let all your thoughts go with the outward breath. Close your eyes and look through your third eye. Think of yourself standing on a beach. The sea is in front of you and you are looking out towards the horizon. It is an early summer's morning and the sky is very clear and blue. You can feel the warmth of the sun on your face and the soft white sand under your bare feet. Listen to the sound of the waves gently breaking and hear the cry of gulls circling over the water. You are alone and feel very peaceful. Step closer to the water, to where the sand is damp, and you will become aware of the slight undertow of the tide tugging at the sand under your feet. Stand here for a minute, and breathe in the odour of the sea.

Now turn to your right and you will see the shore curving round to form a bay. The water there is very shallow and you can see the ribs of sand underneath the gently undulating water. Walk towards the bay and step into the water till it reaches your shins. Feel the icy coolness of it against your skin and the way that the sand shifts under your feet, clouding the waters where you walk. Step back onto dry land and feel the sand sticking to your shins and feet, and how the warmth of the sun dries your skin. Turn so that you are facing away from the sea towards sand dunes. Now climb one. It is steep and your feet plunges into the soft warm sand. Grab hold of grasses to pull yourself up and feel how your muscles work to pull you upwards.

When you reach the top you are a little out of breath, so stop and look at the landscape in front of you. Green fields stretch as far as you can see, rising to gentle hills in the distance. To your right you see a group of ancient, summer lush trees. The grass is soft underfoot and as you look you spot wild flowers growing in clusters. You see red poppies and white meadowsweet. You feel a breeze blow across the side of your face, and you notice how the grass blades bend gently under it in waves. You hear the rustle of leaves in the trees. In the distance a bird swoops over the fields and flies towards the horizon, dwindling to a tiny speck. Inhale the fragrance of the grass and trees, the smell of the earth warming up under the sun.

Now turn to your right and walk towards the trees. Feel the coolness of their shadows as you walk through them and the way the sunlight glances onto your skin through gaps in the branches. From above comes the soft twitter of birds. Sit down at the base of a tree trunk and lean your back against it. Feel the roughness of the bark against your skin and the grass beneath you. Close your eyes and listen to the sounds around you. Relax and just be there for a few minutes. When you are ready, allow your mind to accustom itself to where you really are. Feel the floor under your body, think of where the walls and ceiling are in relation to you, and gradually open your eyes.

You may want to make changes to this journey, perhaps adapting it to fit a landscape that is known to you, or create one of your own. Perhaps you would prefer mountains in the distance, or to begin beside a gushing stream. The important thing is to relax and not worry about details. You don't need to be able to see every blade of grass and whorl of tree bark, just feel the essence of the place and create a sense of spatial awareness as to where things are in relation to you. It might help to record your journey on a cassette and let your voice guide you along.

## Visualisation and the body

Visualisation can be used to stimulate the body as well as withdrawing inside it. Modern medicine is increasingly coming to accept that there is a great deal of truth in the old phrase 'mind over matter'. Intense mental concentration on a body part can actually stimulate a physical response as we know from the work of hypnotists and faith healers, who 'tell' the mind how to respond to a sense impression. However, if you are able to 'tell' your mind how to respond without external assistance, the effect is much increased. A simple demonstration of this fact is to do the lemon test. Close your eyes and think of a ripe yellow lemon. Think of its waxy surface, feel it in your hands. Now take a sharp knife and cut into the fruit. Smell the sharp tang of the lemon juice as you cut yourself a small slice. Now bring it to your mouth, and imagine the scent becoming stronger. Bite into the fruit and feel the juice on your tongue. Now take careful note of what your mouth is actually doing. Yes, it is salivating in response to the idea of that sharp, citrus taste.

Now try concentrating on your scalp, a part of the body that we rarely touch. As you focus intently on that area you will being to feel your nerve-endings tingle. This ability to home in on a part of your body is used in meditation upon the chakras, and can produce amazing results.

## Nidra

Nidra is the name of a meditation exercise wherein you focus on every part of your body in turn to induce a deep state of relaxation, similar to the sensation you feel just before you fall asleep. It is a wonderful exercise to practise at the end of, or even in the middle of, a hectic day, as it will make you feel very refreshed, as if you have had a night's sleep. Begin by lying on your back, in the corpse posture. Make sure that you are comfortable and that you are neither too hot nor too cold. Close your eyes and breath steadily, listening to your breath. You don't need to take deep breaths. Just relax. It can help to imagine that you have entered a zone of non-time. Tell yourself that it will be exactly the same time when you come out of this exercise as you when you began it. Of course it is untrue, but the thought is a very seductive one when you feel that you have been at the mercy of the ticking clock all day.

When you are ready, begin with your scalp. Focus on it till it begins to tingle, and then slowly move your focus down to your forehead. Don't flex and relax as you did for the corpse posture, just concentrate on each area in turn. You will be amazed at how your body reacts, almost as if a warm ray was being shone across it. Keep breathing naturally and gently, and move down your face. Don't think about what each part of your body means to you, or how it looks, just feel it, as if you were occupying the space just inside it. Move down to your shoulders and then focus on each upper arm, each elbow and hand in turn. Move back up to your chest, down your torso to your abdomen, and then down to each thigh, knee and foot in turn. Try to keep your thoughts from wandering off, as this will make you sleepy. The act of concentrating on each part in turn will keep you alert, and you will experience the delicious sensation of being entirely relaxed but awake to enjoy it.

When you are finished, give yourself a moment or two to 'come to', and don't attempt something too urgent or active immediately afterwards. Give yourself time to re-accustom yourself to the world.

## The art of noise

Sounds have a profound effect upon us. They can stimulate deep emotions and even prompt physical responses. Some sounds prompt memories, the strain of a long-forgotten hymn can transport someone back to their schooldays, while the rattle of familiar keys in the lock can make a person feel reassured and happy. However, it is not all to do with memory. Beautiful music can move us to tears or uplift us so that we feel our heart 'soar' with the melody. The sound of waves breaking on a shore induces a sense of peace, while the rumble of thunder makes us alert, perhaps even very nervous. And our recall of sounds is generally much better than we realise. We can learn to recognise someone by the sound of their footsteps, and know instinctively when a sound is 'out of place', such as an unfamiliar creak on a floorboard or a false note in someone's voice.

Concentrating using sound is a viable alternative for anyone who finds visualisation difficult. In some cases, this latter is simply a case of being unable to concentrate fully and will improve with practise. For others, however, it will remain difficult, because the person has a better developed aural memory than a visual one. A way of determining this is to imagine a tennis ball. Picture it, concentrating on its rough texture, its colour and its shape. Keep concentrating until that picture is fully in your mind. Now imagine you have thrown the tennis ball against a wall and it has bounced off and along the pavement. Can you hear it? If you find the listening substantially easier, and more absorbing, than the looking, you may want to try dharana exercises using sound rather than images.

## Hamsa

Hamsa is a Sanskrit word meaning bird, and the hamsa meditation involves visualizing a bird in flight. Take a few deep breaths and fill your mind with the image of a clear blue sky. Now picture a bird soaring across it, watch it swoop and soar across your field of vision. Take a deep breath and as you inhale say the word 'ham', and as you exhale, say 'sa'. Repeat this several times and just allow the bird to fly away, but keep visualizing that sky. Keep up this gentle chanting for several minutes, and you will find that your mind has cleared itself of intruding thoughts and is absorbed by the blue and the notes of the chant.

## Inner sounds (nadas)

Concentrating on inner sounds is another way of shutting out external sounds and thoughts. It also develops increased awareness of your own body and its internal workings. Begin by placing your fingers over your ears; this will shut out external noise. Close your eyes and allow your breathing to relax. As your mind becomes still you will become aware of a steady surging, rumbling sound. In fact, you will be amazed by the noise in there! Keep listening carefully, remembering to keep your body relaxed and your mind focused. Beneath this rumbling sound you will eventually discern subtler sounds. As they become apparent, hone your focus in towards them. If your mind begins to wander, switch back to the louder sounds, then back to the subtler ones behind them. Ultimately your mind will become absorbed by these quieter sounds and you will experience a deep sense of serenity. When you come out of this exercise you may feel surprised at how quiet the outside world is by comparison.

Don't be discouraged if, the first few times you try this, you hear only the surging sounds. Like all yoga techniques, it requires practice and patience.

## Psychic powers

Many yogis claim that yogic meditation can unleash latent psychic powers called Siddhis. However, they warn against the practitioner viewing these powers as an end in themselves as they can lead to pride, which can act as a barrier to the ego-transcendence necessary to achieve samadhi. Certainly regular yoga meditation will help the mind to think more clearly and this will lead to your becoming more perceptive. Whether this will ever lead to your being able to correctly predict the week's lottery numbers is another matter.

One of the powers that yogics claim is that of extrasensory perception (ESP), where a person is able to sense what is about to happen, for instance, when danger is ahead. Modern research has given more credence to the notion of ESP, and researchers in this area have discovered that the deeply meditative state achieved through pratyahara produces the slow Alpha waves that are recognised as being conducive to profound and inspirational thought.

In our normal, waking state our brain activity is characterised by Beta waves. When we are deeply asleep, our brain
activity settles to slower, fainter waves called Delta waves.
However, between waking and sleeping, our brain activity
is characterised by waves that are slower than Beta waves
but much, much stronger. These are called Alpha waves. This
accounts for those unexpected moments of intense lucidity
that we can have before we fall asleep, though we are rarely
able to take advantage of them as our brain is already dip-
ping into Delta wave activity. The Alpha state can, however,
be achieved with conscious effort and people have found
that it gives them access to tremendous insights and ideas.
Modern mind-management gurus often include a guide as
to how to achieve this mindstate in their programmes for
personal success. And their methods are not unlike those
formulated by the yogis all those millennia ago.

## Self-realisation (samadhi)

Once you master the art of focusing on the essence of a thing,
you are ready for the final stage of raja yoga, samadhi. This
is also known as superconsciousness, and is the state wherein
the person meditating feels a oneness with the object of contemplation, and thus with the universe itself. Awareness of
the self is transcended. This is not to say that you become
numb and lacking in awareness. In fact, the opposite is true.
A tremendous sense of peace and wholeness ensues from
this state of 'pure existence'. You are unhampered by conscious thoughts and the intrusion of sense impressions, but
intensely aware of, and merged with, your surroundings.
People who have achieved samadhi describe it as akin to
being filled with dazzling white light. An image not unlike

depictions of visionary saints being by white rays of heavenly light, representing the Holy Spirit entering the human body.

This super-conscious state should not be dismissed as something that only the very religious can achieve. Nor as something from which only such people will benefit. Everyone has a spiritual side to their nature, whether they choose to frame it in religious terms or not, and this heightened state need not interfere with any code of belief, whether it be Hinduism or humanism.

Samadhi could be described as being similar to one of those rare and wonderful moments when we truly 'forget ourselves'. Music and art are often cited as the cause of such transcendent experiences and almost everyone can cite one symphony, song or painting that has, at some time, stopped them in their tracks and lifted them to a state 'beyond words'. Religious music and art especially has this ability to uplift people, perhaps because the creators of it are intensely religious themselves and view their work as a form of worship. Giotto, the thirteenth-century Italian painter, regarded his works as a way of praising God and to this day his famous Assisi frescoes, with their serene, simplistic quality, are capable of imbuing a sense of peace and spiritual hope in those who gaze upon them. John Taverner, the composer whose work was included in the funeral service of Diana, Princess of Wales, is a devout Christian and his work is characterised by a soaring, other-worldly quality that many find truly inspiring.

Like this moments of elation, the state of samadhi does not last. When we come out of it, it is gone, though it can be returned to, and with increasing ease if you continue with dedication. However, samadhi does not leave you empty-handed. It leaves you with the knowledge that such a super-conscious, blissful state is possible, and the realisation that we are not trapped within ourselves and the confines of our daily consciousness.

# Chapter 11

# Other Techniques to Try

### Tactile meditation

Before you begin, choose an object to hold while you are meditating – something light, for if it is too heavy its weight will affect your concentration and hence your ability to focus on it. It need not be particularly soft, but it should not be sharp. Now close your eyes and concentrate on the texture of the object in your hand, focusing on how it feels rather than what it is.

Another method of using touch to help reach the meditative state requires either a set of worry beads or four or five pebbles. Relax in your favourite position, holding the beads or pebbles in the open palm of one hand and with the other move them rhythmically and methodically between your fingers, counting them one at a time.

Feel each bead or pebble as you count, focusing all your attention on the slow, repetitive movement.

### Music and meditation

The relevance of music as an aid to meditation is a personal one. Its effect depends on facilitating your meditations, and that in turn depends on your own instinct and intuition.

Percussion instruments have long been used in meditation,

especially where it is practised by atavists. The music they produce symbolises rhythm and vitality.

Gongs and bells are said to purify the surrounding atmosphere making it more conducive to meditation. Many religions use peals of bells to help their adherents regather wandering thoughts. If you want to use bells as an aid to meditation, focus your thoughts on the sound, trying to experience it beyond audibility.

Harps have long been associated with meditation. In China the cheng and other zither-like instruments are widely used, while in India, the sitar and the vina accompany meditative chanting.

The gentle tinkling of the Aeolian harp can create a perfectly calm state of mind as you approach your meditations, and help you to focus your thought.

To meditate to music, take up your usual position, close your eyes and listen to a favourite piece, immersing yourself in it completely. Try to become one with the music, letting the sound encompass you. If you find that your thoughts are invaded by memories associated with the piece that you have selected, imagine them as musical notes floating off into the distance.

## Zen meditation

The word 'Zen' derives from the Sanskrit dhyana, meaning 'meditation'. With its roots in the Yisuddhimagga tradition, it is widely practised in Japan, having arrived there through the Ch'an meditation school of China.

Zen's main practice is zazen, or sitting on a cushion facing a wall, and is done daily by those who practise it, usually adopting the full lotus position. Meditation sessions are quite lengthy, hence, in zazen, great stress is placed on correct posture. The body is held upright, and it should be theoretically possible to draw a line from the centre of the forehead down through the nose, chin, throat, navel into the coccyx at the tail of the spine. Every part of the body must be in balance: if it is not, incorrect balance in one part of the body will cause strain in another and ruin the meditation.

The left hand rests within the right, the middle joints of the middle fingers touching, with the thumbs, also lightly touching each other, held at the navel and the arms slightly away from the rest of the body.

Apart from the fact that novices to Zen are sometimes advised to count their breaths, from one to ten, and the use of koan (*see* below), zazen uses no mantra, mandala or other object of meditation. In zazen, thoughts are allowed to come and go without being banished by the meditator, who remains attentive and alert throughout the meditation, concentrating on sitting as still as possible in a state of quiet awareness.

## Koan

Zen masters often ask their pupils impenetrable questions, known as koan, an unanswerable puzzle designed to precipitate awakening by breaking through the limited confines of consciousness. A common one is 'What was your face before you were born?' From then on, whenever the koan comes to mind, the pupil banishes all other thoughts and concentrates on his koan. As he comes to realise that there is no answer per se, he reaches a state that has been described by those who have achieved it as 'feverish concentration', from which arises 'supreme frustration', and with conscious thought transcended, the pupil attains samadhi, the state of total concentration.

The first koan is said to have arisen when the great Zen master Hui-neng was attacked by robbers. He begged them to be silent for a moment and then said to them, 'When you are thinking of neither good nor evil, what is at that moment your original face?' The assailants were so astonished that they begged Hui for an explanation. The master sent them on their way, and the men found that the question came to dominate their thoughts to such an extent that when something else came to mind, they banished it and resumed their meditation on the question until they found they had arrived at samadhi.

# Chapter 12

# Yoga: The Six Paths and the Eight Limbs

### The six paths of yoga

Samadhi, or self-realisation, can be reached by six different strands of yoga, though some are less open to secular interpretation than others. There is, however, no requirement to subscribe to all six paths.

### Bhakti yoga

Bhakti yoga is characterised by devotion. To achieve the ultimate goal, the *Bhakti* practitioner must meditate upon the supreme being, and behave unselfishly towards his or her fellow man. As in countless religions, yoga advocates that you love your neighbour; a universal message for promoting harmony. Most of us are already aware of the inner sense of joy engendered by doing completely unselfish acts.

### Gyana yoga

Gyana (or jnana) yoga is concerned with wisdom, and urges the study of texts as well as a deep consideration of the questions of life, such as who we are and why we are here. Followers are pointed towards the *Bhagavad Gita* and other sacred texts, to search for meaning therein, just as medieval monks poured over the gospels, seeking new insights.

### Karma yoga

Karma yoga is the yoga of actions. Just as Giotto held that his frescoes were, in themselves, an act of worship, so the karma subscriber seeks to praise his creator through thought and deed, and to regard his or her work as an act of worship.

### Mantra yoga

Mantra yoga utilises sound and is discussed in Chapter 8.

### Hatha yoga

Hatha yoga is the only physical yoga and the one that this section mostly concentrates upon. It is the strand that most people take up first, or indeed, exclusively. Hatha yoga seeks to strengthen the inner as well as outer body, that is, the internal organs as well as the external muscles, and to focus the mind through physical activity.

Hatha yoga is considered by some as merely the necessary preliminary to raja yoga. The idea is that the body must be at its healthiest and strongest if you are to achieve transcendence. This does not, however, mean that your body must conform to an ideal of physical beauty, but that it should be as good as it can be. Thus disability or age need not be a hindrance.

### Raja yoga

This path of yoga has been discussed in Chapter 9.

All six yogas seek to unite the self and the universe. Though they may look solitary, the text studying and the silent repetition of mantras, they produce a sense of belonging that is the very antithesis of solitude.

## The eight limbs of yoga

Most people who take up yoga find that, after a while, it begins to have an effect upon their lifestyle and codes of behaviour, as they begin to take more and more control of their destinies. The eight limbs of yoga, first spelled out in Pantajali's *Yoga Sutras*, provide guidelines for yoga lifestyle as well as practice.

The limbs are abstinences (yamas), observances (niyamas), postures (asanas), breath control (pranayama), withdrawal of senses (pratyahara), concentration (dharana), meditation (dhyana) and self-realisation (samadhi).

It is important to be aware that yoga is not a system cast in stone. Adapt its ideas to suit your own, just as you will learn to adapt the postures of hatha yoga to suit your levels of strength and suppleness.

## The abstinences (yamas)
### Nonviolence (ahisma)
The first of these is the principle of nonviolence (ahisma), which is not merely a directive to not administer bodily pain. You may be someone who has never raised their hand to anyone, but be violent with words, wreaking emotional rather than physical havoc. You may be violent towards the environment, doing your bit to spread pollution, or violent towards yourself, either in extreme forms, such as self-mutilation, or in self-destructive habits, such as bulimia nervosa, or alcoholism.

Ahisma is not a passive principle; indeed, it can require

enormous creativity and energy finding nonviolent ways to achieve ends that may previously have been reached with violence, or the threat of it.

### Truthfulness (satya)

The second yama is that of truthfulness (satya). This is not just about not telling lies, but about living with integrity. This can mean not talking about someone behind their back and being honest about personally held convictions. It does not mean speaking your mind, however cruelly, in the manner of the Jim Carrey character in the film *Liar, Liar* (which tells the story of a lawyer who suddenly loses his ability to deal in half-truths and cannot stop himself from blurting out exactly what he thinks, no matter what the situation). There are times when a white lie is actually more honourable than a truth.

### Non-stealing (asteya)

Next is non-stealing (asteya), which is against taking any-thing that is not rightfully yours, including the credit for something you do not deserve, or stealing someone's time, by demanding their attention and support to an unfair de-gree. Only you can judge when the line has been crossed. All yoga principles leave the responsibility firmly up to the individual, which may at first seem like a burden, but is, in fact, incredibly liberating.

### Continence (bramachanya)

The fourth yama is that of continence (bramachanya). This is often interpreted as meaning celibacy, which it does not; rather it is a principle of moderation in all things. Avoid be-ing the slave of your desires. The 1990s saw the concept of addiction as a disease hit the headlines. Unfortunately, the underlying message in these media stories is that addicts cannot control themselves, whether their addiction be to Class A drugs or having sex with strangers. Yoga does not accept this; you are in charge of your appetites and it is your job to keep a rein on them. It goes without saying that you should avoid tempting others to overindulge themselves either.

### Non-possessiveness (aparigrapha)

The final yama is non-possessiveness (aparigrapha), and it requires you to free yourself from materialism. In the 1980s, many people discovered that materialism did not make them happy. Indeed, many found the opposite to be the case, as they substituted the pursuit of wealth for other values, leaving them with a feeling of emptiness despite their materialistic ambitions being realised. Aparigrapha does not require the relinquishing of comfort and wealth, simply that you begin to value it less highly and turn your attention to less worldly matters.

The principle also requires living without envying what others have, whether it be acres of land or a perfect hourglass figure.

## The observances (niyamas)

### Purity (saucha)

Purity (saucha) requires the cleanliness of the internal and external body, as well as of the mind. Before practising yoga postures, you are advised to shower and wear clean clothes. To cleanse the inner body, yogics advised a pure (sattvic) diet and pranayama, a system of breathing that helps to clean out the system.

Purifying the mind is an altogether more difficult matter, as it involves the clearing out of old resentments and prejudices, just as you would clear out an old cupboard. However, like the cupboard, a cleared-out mind has acres of room for new ideas and progress. Modern therapy practices agree with the idea that mental detritus hinders clear thought and can stop you from moving forward in life, and that unresolved emotions can fester and become deeply negative. For instance, unresolved anger can turn into bitterness, isolation and insecurity.

In future, resolve to deal with emotional situations as they arise, and avoid repeating behavioural patterns that result in negative feelings. This does not mean flying off the handle, but recognising strong emotions such as anger, and choosing how to respond. Nor does it mean cowering away from life, but simply recognising and avoiding destructive situations.

## Contentment (santosha)

Contentment (santosha) urges you to be happy with your lot, to rid yourself of desires and accept the hand that fate has dealt you. If this sounds like an invitation to abdicate responsibility for the direction your life will take, consider it another way. The ancients were well aware that bad days came as often as good ones, that no-one who ever lived avoided at least some tragedy and unhappiness. Santosha would be better seen as an acknowledgement of each moment that makes up your life. After all, not one of them will come again, and even bad times are unique. Also, there is no peace to be found in denying or resisting pain.

Consider the story of Jean-Dominique Bauby, one-time

editor of French *Elle*, who, following a stroke, became a victim of 'locked-in' syndrome, a debility which robbed him of all faculties of movement and speech. He wrote an account of his illness, and his coming to terms with it, called *The Diving Bell and The Butterfly*, by dictating it letter for letter using the movement of his eyelashes by way of communication. By accepting his new state, living with it rather than railing mentally against it, Bauby came to find a sense of profound peace. Had he instead continued to compare his present to his past, he would have experienced the remainder of his life as a period of unmitigated torment.

Santosha also advises against denying your present through daydreaming and fantasy; 'wishing your life away', in other words. Far better to be fully alive to your life as it happens.

### Austerity (tapas)
Austerity (tapas) has nothing to do with horsehair shirts or kneeling on cold stone floors, but is merely the observance of discipline and simplicity. Such a lifestyle will assist you in sticking to your purpose, rather than being snared by the distractions of a complicated existence. The novelist Anne Fine, author of *Mrs Doubtfire*, described, in an interview in *The Guardian*, the moment she realised how to achieve success as a writer. She was changing the bedsheets one day, and happened to be listening to a play on the radio. One of the actors said the words 'Simplify, simplify', and she realised that this was what she needed to do with her life. From that day forth, she filtered out all the unnecessary little tasks that used up her energy and thoughts and devoted herself to what she truly burned to do.

The word 'tapas' comes from 'tap', meaning to burn or

blaze. Observance of tapas will allow your inner light to burn all the more brightly.

## Study (svadhyaya)

Study (svadhyaya) requires the study of life and its meaning, and any study or activity that increases knowledge of the self. This latter could include voluntary work or spending time with the elderly or children, interacting with the world in such a way that untried, even unsuspected, aspects of the self are brought out. It also requires a certain degree of solitariness and thoughtfulness, giving you time to listen to how your own mind ticks, as well as to contemplate the workings of the world around you.

## Attentiveness to the divine (ishvara pranidhana)

Attentiveness to the divine (ishvara pranidhana) is the transcending of the ego, as you seek to become one with the supreme being. To achieve this, short-termism must be abandoned in favour of the long-term, your energies and thoughts devoted to the pursuit of love, progress and creation, Ishvara, not dissipated by day-to-day issues and wants.

The asanas will be detailed in Chapter 13, while pranayama and the final four limbs of yoga are explained in Chapter 10, which looks at advanced meditation techniques.

# Chapter 13

# The Hatha Postures (Asanas)

The following chapter is a how-to-do guide for each hatha posture, called an asana. Do not expect to be able to do them all at the first attempt, and remember that it is more important to be able to do a few of them well, than all of them badly. Pay particular attention to the warm-up and relaxation (corpse posture) exercises, on pages 63–70 as these must be included in your daily sessions. After all, you would not embark on an aerobics session without first allowing yourself a few minutes preparation and no more should you neglect this part of a yoga session. Even though it seems the gentlest of exercises, you are about to give your muscles a serious workout.

Remember too that it is important to balance each asana with its symmetrical opposite. For every forward stretch, do a backward one, a stretch to the left followed by a stretch to the right and so on. This ensures that every muscle you flex is given the opportunity to relax.

If you suffer from high blood pressure, have any heart problems, or are menstruating, omit the inverted postures, such as the shoulder and head stands. If you are at all unsure about the wisdom of attempting anything vis-a-vis your state of health it is imperative that you seek the advice of your doctor. In almost all cases, however, doctors will be delighted by your initiative.

Do not be discouraged by any ideas that yoga is for slim people only. Being overweight may make some of the exercises difficult but do not lose heart; in time you will gradually master them. Many overweight people who have tried yoga have found it to be a gateway to other exercises as regular practice increases their flexibility and muscular strength. The added bonus is that yoga can help people overcome weight problems. Not only does it tone muscles, leading to a more slender physique, it can lead you to a more balanced and healthy approach to diet. Those who have lived a very sedentary lifestyle will also find that yoga rejuvenates them and increases their appetite for physical exercise.

The first time you try some of these asanas you may find them uncomfortable. If so, do not torture yourself by holding them for any length of time. Hard as it may be to believe, these postures will one day come to seem very comfortable! Keep this book handy at all times and study the postures over and over again to ensure that you are doing them correctly. If you are unsure, look for a teacher to guide you on the finer points and use this book as a backup for yoga practice at home.

## Diaphragm breathing

To fully benefit from any yoga exercise it is helpful to breathe properly using the diaphragm as opposed to the chest. The diaphragm is the long flat muscle situated at the bottom of your lungs. To locate it, place your hand on your stomach, just below your ribs, and cough. You will feel a muscle tremble underneath your hand: this is your diaphragm. Now, keeping your hand where it is, repeat that coughing action slowly, but this time without restricting the flow of air from your throat, which you do when you cough. You will feel that a column of air is being pushed up through your body and that your diaphragm is contracting as it rises in accordance. Inhale deeply and you will feel the diaphragm expand as it lowers. Try holding a dictionary, or similar weight object, above your head. As you breathe you will be able to feel the diaphragm rising and falling. Focus on breathing using this muscle alone, remembering to keep your chest in and your shoulders down.

Opera singers and wind instrument musicians are well aware of the power of diaphragm breathing. Without it they would not be able to produce long, pure notes with their voices or control the volume and purity of sound from, for example, a clarinet. Short, weak breaths produce only warbling songs and ghastly clarinet squeaks! Next time you watch Pavarotti perform, note how his chest does not rise or fall with his voice; the air that is powering his voice is being pumped up by his diaphragm.

Breathing in this way stimulates the solar plexus, the network of nerves that supply the abdominal area which is situated in what we refer to as the 'pit of the stomach'. A good supply of oxygen to this area will keep the inner organs, such as the kidneys and pancreas, functioning efficiently, which is clearly good for all-over health. It is here also that the manipura chakra is situated (*see* page 249 for more information). According to yogic wisdom, it is from here that the life-force stems, the 'inner fire' that pushes us forward in life. Think of it as a fire that needs air to burn brightly. Shallow breathing will leave it sputtering and weak. It is this area that we refer to when we talk about a 'gut feeling', an instinct so strong that we feel it as opposed to just thinking it, and therefore tend to trust it more. Good yogic breathing will help to sharpen up your instincts too.

Diaphragm breathing requires a lot of practice in order to be able to do it without thinking. You do not need to restrict your practice of it to yoga sessions. Try doing it at odd moments throughout the day, until it becomes second nature.

## Mindfulness

Mindfulness is the mindstate wherein we become very aware of our own self and the world around us. When we talk about 'living in the moment' we are referring to instances where we sink into an experience, and live it fully. This is not to be confused with the notion of recklessness, where caution and responsibility is thrown to the wind, but rather a moment when every channel of receptivity, every sense, is fully alert, and we are alive to the richness inherent in even the most mundane moment. In his poem 'Stopping By Woods On A Snowy Evening', the American poet Robert Frost describes just such a moment on a dark and cold night when he interrupts a long journey, and his cycle of conscious thought, to gaze at the forest: 'The only sound's the sweep/Of easy wind and downy flake./The woods are lovely dark and deep.' The reader can almost feel the stillness and serenity in which the poet basks before pulling himself back to the task in hand: 'But I have promises to keep/And miles to go before I sleep.'

The teachings of Zen Buddhism advocate the same principle of alertness to the immediate. Only by learning to surrender ourselves, if only once in a while, to the here and now can we appreciate the beauty of the universe and truly live. Next time you are washing the dishes try a little Zen. Clear your mind of all stray thoughts and tune into the moment by concentrating on what you are doing to the exclusion of all else. Really feel the temperature of the water, focus on the soapy bubbles, the action of your hands and how the dirt lifts from the dishes. Listen fully to the scrape of cutlery against the side of the basin. When you come out of your reverie, you will feel refreshed and probably discover that you have done a spanking job on those dishes. And you never know, you may even come to find the experience of washing-up quite a pleasurable and relaxing one.

This is the state of mindfulness to which yogic teachings refer, and which can greatly enhance the effectiveness of the hatha postures. When doing your daily yoga session, try to do them in the Zen manner described above, focusing on how your body feels and what you are doing. Eventually this habit of tuning in to what you are doing will filter into your daily life, greatly enriching it.

## Sitting, standing and lying positions

Lay out your blanket or mat, ensure that you are wearing nothing that is constricting, and begin by sitting down cross-legged. If this is too much of a strain on your thighs then prop up each knee with a cushion. Feeling uncomfortable will only sabotage your chances of relaxing. If this is still a strain, stretch your legs out in front of your body, about shoulders' width apart, with knees bent. You might want the further support of a folded-up blanket to sit on. Try not to be disheartened by difficulties as your aches and pains will begin to ease up.

Make sure that your weight is not resting on the base of your spine but on your pelvic bone. The shape of your abdomen will tell you if you are sitting correctly as it should be long and straight, not squashed and curved inwards. Straighten your back, lift your head and relax your shoulders. Imagine that there is a piece of string attached to the crown of your head, lifting it slightly towards the ceiling, but not so much that your spine 'locks' – you are not on military parade. Place your hands, palms upward, lightly upon your knees. Take a deep breath and exhale slowly. As you breathe try to focus on your body and how it feels. Let your diaphragm rise and fall naturally with your breath.

Now imagine that each intake of breath as clean, white light and each outward breath as grey and smoky. Think of the white light as forcing out the tensions and niggles that have gathered inside you during the day; breathe out that meeting, that traffic jam, that overdraft, and breathe in a mountain stream.

Allow yourself as long as you need to thoroughly focus on what you are doing, where you are and how your body feels. This is your very own time; allow yourself to sink into it. The world can wait.

Once you are relaxed, give your arms a little stretch and slowly stand up.

## Beginning the session
Remember, before beginning a routine of asanas it is important that you complete the warm-up exercise described on pages 63–70 in Chapter 4.

## The Asanas
### The mountain (tadasana)
Begin by waking up your feet. Stand on tiptoe a couple of times, then return them flat to the floor. Give your toes a good wriggle to get the blood moving and then stand with

your feet together and your spine straight. Keep your knees loose by concentrating on lifting the muscles above them. Check that your abdomen is straight, not bulging out or curving in, and tuck in your buttocks. Let your hands, palms in, rest on the sides of your thighs.

Take a deep breath and relax your shoulders and open your chest. Remember the string between the crown of your head and the ceiling, and allow your facial muscles to relax. Breathe naturally and feel how your body maintains its balance, feel the space around you and the floor under your feet. This is best done with your eyes closed. You will become aware of every muscle and tendon, and this awareness will gradually filter into your general consciousness resulting in a wonderfully improved posture. Standing and walking erect will not only make you appear slimmer and more dynamic,

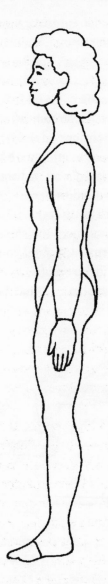

*The mountain*

it will also improve your all-over health by allowing you to breathe more efficiently.

*The cat*
This asana evolved from studying the movements of cats as they lazily stretch after a nap, or interrupt a walk to take give their legs an energizing flex, and it helps to think of the way a cat would move when mastering this movement. It is also a great way of waking up your whole body as it boosts the circulation.

Kneel on all fours with your hands a shoulders' width apart and your knees the same distance apart as your hands. Keep your arms straight throughout the entire exercise if you can. Take a deep breath and, as you exhale, move your chin down to your chest so that you are looking down towards your

*The cat*

abdomen. Arch your back, making your shoulders round and keeping your buttocks down. Your spine should now be stretched into a very gentle C-shape.

As you inhale, hollow your back into a concave position and lift your head, curving your neck and shoulders upwards. Your spine should now form a shallow inverted C-shape. Repeat these two positions five to ten times, concentrating on creating a slow fluid movement. Think slow languorous cat, not bucking bronco, throughout!

### The cat (advanced)
From the starting position for the cat, take a deep breath, exhale and arch your back. This time, however, take your right knee and bring it forward towards your forehead. Bring your forehead down to meet it.

*The cat (advanced)*

On the inhale, hollow your back as before, with your head curved up, and push your right leg back and up as far as you can go. Do not kick your leg back. Return to the starting position and repeat for the left leg. Repeat three to four times each, or until you feel tired. This is a very vigorous asana so it requires quite a lot of physical strength to keep the movement fluid and controlled.

### The canoe

This is a good exercise for toning the abdominal muscles, as well as the spine. Begin by lying on your front with your arms stretched out in front of you, your legs stretched out behind with the backs of the feet making contact with the floor, and your chin resting on the floor. Keep your hands and feet shoulders'-width apart.

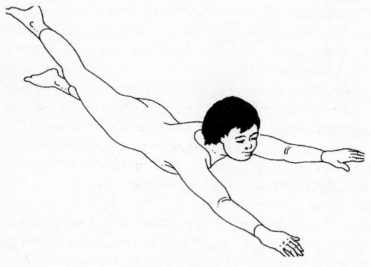

*The canoe*

Take a deep breath and as you inhale, lift your right leg and your left arm and stretch them both out straight. Allow your head to move upwards but not so far as to stretch your neck. Try to keep your left hip and right shoulder in contact with the floor. As you exhale, slowly lower your arm and leg to the floor. Inhale and do the same wit the left leg and right arm. Do not hold the position for so long that you cannot help but collapse under the strain. Repeat three times for each side.

And now for the full canoe, which you only have to do twice. Take a deep, deep breath and lift both arms and both legs, keeping them straight as before. Your weight should be centred on your abdomen. Hold, then exhale, lowering yourself gently to the ground.

### The triangle (trikonasana)

There are two versions of this, the first being easier to attain than the second. Begin by standing with your feet slightly more than shoulders'-width apart and the palms of your hands flat against the sides of your thighs. Lift your right arm straight up so that it is brushing against your right ear. Breathe in and bend to the left. Let your right arm lead and pull you over while your left hand, sliding down your thigh, offers support. Do not, however, lean your weight into your left arm. Try to stretch far enough for your right arm to make a right angle with your legs and keep your face and hips facing forward.

This not only stretches your spine, it also stretches the muscles of your chest and waist too. As you exhale, move slowly back into the standing position and repeat for the other side. Repeat three times each way.

*The triangle*

The second triangle requires you to stretch without the assistance of the pulling arm. Begin by standing upright and stretch out your arms to either side so that they are parallel with the floor. Extend the right foot to the right hand side and, as you exhale, bend over towards the right so that your right hand slides down your thigh in the direction of the ankle. There should be no forward inclination of the body at this time. As the bending action takes place, your left arm should be lifted upright with the palm of the hand facing forward. Your right leg, right arm and torso should now form a triangle. This stretch should be maintained for the minimum of a minute. Try to extend the stretch as you exhale. You will find that if you rest for a second and then try again to extend, your body will give a little more. As you inhale, return slowly to an upright position, and repeat the stretch to the left upon the inhale. Repeat three times for each side.

To keep the movement fluid, think of your spine as a piece of elastic being stretched lengthwise as well as sideways. But take care not to ping back too abruptly. When done properly, this is a very calming exercise, partly because it requires such intense concentration. It is also very beneficial in speeding up the expulsion of toxins from the body as it tones the pancreas and kidneys, helping them to operate more efficiently.

*The tree (vrksasasana)*
This is a classic meditative, or praying, pose. You sometimes see drawings and photographs of Hindus praying in this one-legged posture, as it is an excellent way of focusing the mind. Mastery of it will make you feel like a real Yogi! Its other benefits include improved balance and posture, and makes your aware of the importance of evenly distributing your body weight be-

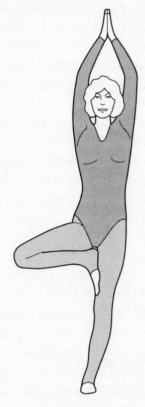

*The tree*

tween toes and heels. You might like to use the chair for support initially as good balance is required.

Begin in the tadasana, focusing your eyes on a spot in front of you. Remember to keep focusing as this will help you to maintain your balance throughout the exercise. Shift your weight onto your right foot. Make sure that you are using your entire foot, as balancing on your heel or toes is guaran-

185

teed to have your toppling over. Now place the sole of your left foot onto the inside of your right knee. You can use your hands to help. Allow the left knee to relax – it does not need to stick out at right angles to the body. If you need to hold onto the chair, do so. If not, bring the palms of your hands together at chest height, as if you were about to pray. Take a deep breath, close your eyes, and feel how your body balances itself on one leg. It might help to actually think of a tree, rooted into the earth. Many people find this mental image makes them feel surprisingly secure. Hold for as long as is comfortable and then lift your left foot back onto the floor. Repeat the process for the other leg, and then repeat three times for each side.

Once that you feel secure with this asana, try placing your left foot as high up on your thigh as possible. Again, allow the knee to slope down naturally. Raise your arms above your head, stretched to their fullest extent, and bring the palms together. Enjoy the stretch and relax. If you think too much about losing your balance it becomes a self-fulfilling prophecy. Also, if you worry about it, your fall will be all the more painful as your muscles will be tense, and the soothing effect of the exercise will elude you.

### The cobra (bhujangasana)

'Bhujanga' means serpent and the asana that bears its name resembles that of a cobra rearing up to strike. It is a posture that stretches the chest and abdomen. Do not bend so far back that you cannot prevent yourself from collapsing forward; this should be an easy, natural movement.

Begin by lying face downwards on the floor with your hands under your shoulders and your elbows bent. As if you were about to do a press-up except that your feet are flat, not tucked in at the toes. Keep your feet together throughout the exercise. Inhale deeply and, making sure that your hips and legs remain in contact with the floor, slowly lift up your head and upper body, so that your back is curved, your chin facing the ceiling and your arms straight. Do not allow your shoulders to hunch up towards your ears.

Hold for a short period, focusing your attention on the small of your back and the proud sinuous curve of your chest and neck. Slowly relax, lowering your torso, then your chin, nose and forehead, to the floor. To increase the spinal stretch, keep the arms close by your side and move the palms closer together on the floor. To reduce the stretch, vice versa, and allow the elbows to bend.

This exercise helps to tone the abdomen and buttocks, and speed up the elimination of fat from the waist and hips. It is particularly beneficial to women as it increases the blood

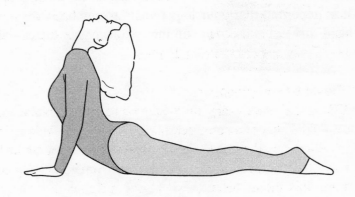

*The cobra*

supply to internal organs including the ovaries and uterus and can help to regulate the menstrual cycle. It is also useful in combating digestive and kidney problems.

### The forward bend (paschimotanasana)

A backward stretch should always be followed, or preceded, by a forward stretch, to allow the abdominal and chest muscles to contract. The forward bend stretches the entire back of the body, from the neck to the knees, and requires a fair amount of suppleness. However, as always, you are the judge of how much of a stretch you can cope with. In Sanskrit, the word 'Paschima' means West. Traditionally, you would face the East for all your yogic exercises, and therefore your body would be getting stretched on its Western side.

Sit with your legs stretched out in front of you, knees very straight, and feet together. Inhale and stretch your arms above your head. Exhale very slowly and smoothly bend forward from the hips (not the waist) to grasp your toes. If, at first, this seems difficult, reach for your ankles, calves or knees. It is important that your legs remain straight. Continue to bend forward and down, aiming to touch your knees with

*The forward bend*

your forehead. Hold for at least ten seconds and observe your breath. Release the hold and very slowly unroll your spine, returning to a sitting position.

The forward bend slows the respiratory rate to produce a calm and relaxed state of mind. It also increases the suppleness of the spine and improves blood circulation in the abdomen, improving digestion and the health of the female reproductive organs.

The more supple may like to begin the forward bend from a lying down position. From here, the aim is to lift the upper body, unaided and without jerking, while keeping your legs flat on the ground.

### The bow (dhanurasana)

This posture resembles a drawn bow and it helps when performing it to think on the curved tautness of the wood. To begin, lie flat on the floor with your arms by your sides and your legs flat. Keeping your thighs on the floor, raise your knees so that they touch the buttocks and reach for your ankles with your hands. Take a deep breath and as you exhale, pull with your hands to lift your legs as high as possible, while arching the front of your body and raising your chin up towards the ceiling. Remember the slow curve of the bow and try not to do this movement in a single, sudden jerk. Keep your toes pointed away from your body and your heels pointed towards your head. Your weight should be centred on your abdomen. Try to keep your legs together but if this is too much of a strain, you may need to begin with your legs apart. Hold this pose and the outward breath and then, as you inhale, relax into your original position.

This stretch is great for the spine, making it more flexible

*The bow*

and strong. Because it stretches the whole front of the body, it also has a spectacular effect on posture as it loosens up the accumulated tensions created by stooped shoulders and a slouched stance. The energizing effect this has will make you want to walk tall. The bow also tones inner organs and is especially good for liver and kidney health and promoting efficient digestion.

### The bridge (satu bhandasana)
This posture is very soothing and give the abdomen and thighs a really good stretch. Begin by lying on your back with your arms by your side and your legs slightly apart. Bend your knees and bring your heels in beside your buttocks. Support your hips with your hands and, as you take a deep inward breath, lift your torso and thighs till they

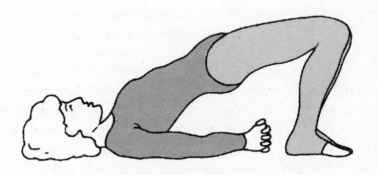

*The bridge*

form a line. Now move your hands to support your lower back, remembering to play the fingers for maximum support. Lift your spine between your shoulder blades and relax your facial muscles. When you are comfortable and feel that the pose is stable, remove your hands and lay your arms our flat, linking the fingers underneath your body.

For an extra stretch, incline your body as far as it will go to the right without lifting your shoulders from the floor. Return slowly to the centre and then incline towards the left. To make the bridge a little bigger, pressure can be exerted by bracing the arms and feet. Try not to squeeze your shoulder with your upper arms when doing this. Hold this position for at least a minute and then allow yourself to sink slowly back onto the floor.

## The wheel (chakrasana) (16)

A more advanced version of the bridge is the wheel, which you may also recognise as the 'crab'. This posture gives the whole frontal body a good stretch but should not be attempted until you are comfortable with the previous exercise.

As before, begin by lying on your back, with your knees bent and your feet flat on the floor. Now place your hands, palms downward, on either side of your head with the fingertips facing your feet. Lift your buttocks slightly and feel your weight being borne equally by your hands and feet. Take a deep breath and, as you inhale, raise your torso till your back is fully arched. Tuck your head in so that you face the floor. Hold this pose for only a few seconds at first. It is a very dynamic and athletic stance and is more tiring than it looks. Do not let yourself become so exhausted that you crash back onto the floor. Instead, when you are ready to come down, bring your head back so that it faces out the way, and gently stretch your neck. Allow your spine to slowly uncurl down onto the floor.

For the truly gymnastic there is a rocking movement to the wheel. While your back is fully arched, try leaning towards the front of the body. Allow the weight to transfer from your feet to your hands. You must be in total control of this movement otherwise you will collapse forward, so take care not to lean so far that your chest is projecting further than your elbows. Hold for a very short period and then slowly rock back to your original wheel position, returning half your weight to the soles of your feet.

Both the bridge and the wheel are excellent for reducing bloating and aiding digestive efficiency. They are also powerful allies in the battle of the bulge as they tone the abdo-

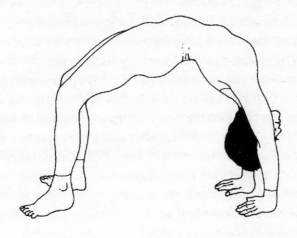

*The wheel*

men. And last but not least, having mastered the wheel you can congratulate yourself on having regained some of your childhood suppleness.

To relax your abdomen after these exercises, lie on your back and bring your knees up to your chest. Hold the knees lightly with your hands and enjoy the sensation of those hard-working muscles contracting.

### The spinal twist (matsyendrasana)
The last two exercises are of enormous benefit to preventing back trouble as they strengthen and flex the spine. This next asana, and its variations, will also strengthen the back. Lower back twinges will gradually diminish thanks, in great part, to this particular posture, so long as it is done correctly. Throughout this exercise concentrate on relaxing and mov-

ing slowly and fluidly. After all, sudden jerks can be extremely painful, as anyone who has ever done given their back 'a nasty turn' will tell you. The subsequent misery could put you off yoga for a long time.

Begin by sitting on the floor with your legs in front of you. The backs of your heels should be on the floor with your toes facing up the way while your back is straight. As with the sitting position at the very beginning, do not sit up too stiffly but as if the crown of your head were being pulled slightly in the direction of the ceiling. Bend the right leg and lift it over the left leg at the knee. Use your left hand to support your upper body by placing it behind you, palm down, at the centre of your spine. Avoid putting any weight on this hand if you can.

Place your right hand on the floor beside your left thigh. Take a deep breath and, as you exhale, twist your upper body

*The spinal twist*

to the left, leading with your head, but letting your shoulders do the pulling work. Keep your buttocks and legs firmly on the ground. Try to twist a little further round upon the second exhale. Hold for perhaps a minute then slowly resume your starting position. Repeat this movement for the other side. It is important to relax during this movement in order to keep it fluid, and to make the most of this asana's gift for promoting a sense of psychological balance.

Once you have learnt the spinal twist you are ready to attempt it with the legs bent. Begin as before, then bend your right leg in and under so that the foot is making contact with the groin area. Keep the whole leg on the floor if possible. Bend your left leg and bring your foot so that it rests on the floor on the outside right of your right knee. Again, place your left hand behind your back, remembering not to lean on it. Now take your right arm and crook it so that the elbow is on the outside left of the upraised left knee. The hand can either be raised with the fingers together, resting lightly on your waist or holding onto your left ankle. Turn to look over your left shoulder, keeping your shoulders relaxed and avoiding putting too much strain on the neck muscles. Hold then return to the original position. Repeat for the other side.

This exercise tones the abdomen and is good for internal organs. It is also very beneficial to the nervous system enabling it to function efficiently.

### The fish (matsyasana) (2)

This is best performed after the shoulder-stand as it releases any tensions in the shoulders and neck. It also improves circulation, particularly to the head, thereby stimulating the brain and giving the complexion a boost. Anyone prone to bronchial or other lung-related ailments will benefit from the fish as it works the lungs, expanding their capacity.

Begin by lying on your back with your legs straight out in front of you and your feet together. Arch your back, keeping your buttocks firmly on the ground. Use your elbows (with the forearms and palms flat on the floor) to support you. Allow the head to drop back until the crown is in contact with the floor. This will probably require you to slide your elbows away from the body a little. You should now be really feeling the expansion in your chest. Your weight should be distributed between the crown of the head and the buttocks.

Once you feel relaxed and confident in this pose you can remove your elbows from their propping position. Bring the palms together at chest level, as if you were praying, and close your eyes and hold. Breathe calmly and naturally. Re-

*The fish*

turn to your original position by slowly lowering your arms so that they support you again, untuck your head and roll your spine down to the floor.

Once your strength increases you might like to try leg-lifting during this movement, as this will give your thighs and abdomen a wonderfully effective toning session. While in the 'praying' position, take a deep breath. As you inhale, raise your right leg a little distance from the floor. The nearer your foot to the ground, the tougher the exercise. Do not let your leg swing up to a 90-degree angle from the floor. Your leg may be a little shaky the first time so do not hold for long. Slowly lower it as you exhale and repeat for the other side.

### The rabbit (3)

This is another good exercise for the lungs. In fact, it virtually constitutes an all-over lung workout. It is so-called because of its resemblance to the postures of a rabbit, though you will obviously be seeking to avoid the sudden bucking motions associated with this creature when it takes fright and runs.

Begin by sitting on your heels with your feet flat on the ground. Lean forward so that your chest makes contact with your thighs, your head is facing forward and your forearms flat on the ground, palms down. Retain this pose and breathe consciously from the diaphragm, noting how the inhalation of oxygen causes your abdomen to swell, while exhalation causes it to contract. This is a very comforting pose and makes you feel very tucked in and secure. If you feel an unpleasant strain on your thighs, then lift your upper body till you are more comfortable.

Next, sit up so that your hand are palms down in front of your knees and your arms are straight. As before, focus on your abdomen as it responds to inhalation and exhalation. Take several deep breaths before moving on to the next stage, which resembles a rabbit trying to manoeuvre itself into a headstand! Bring your head, crown first, down onto the floor. You might want to move your hands a little further forward to give your head and shoulders some support. Again, listen to your breathing. As you breathe in think of pure oxygen being sucked into your lungs, forcing out stale clouds of old air. Think of it as opening a window on a smoky room; feel your lungs becoming as fresh as the clean outside air. Hold this pose for a short period before returning to a sitting position.

Initially, the inverted posture of the head should only be held for a short time. The good news is that such an exercise

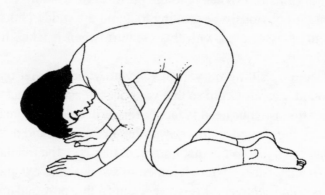

*The rabbit*

stimulates the thyroid and pituitary glands as well as the brain. Many yoga practitioners claim that exercises involving the inversion of the head lead to better powers of concentration, improved memory and the ability to grasp complicated concepts. It is also thought to help ward off senility.

### The dog (7)

Yoga, like many modern fitness regimes, subscribes to the notion that if you 'don't use it, you'll lose it'. So, while it is important to stretch and work the spine, do not forget to include a few asanas that work other areas. The dog is good for toning and strengthening the calves and ankles as well as giving the back and shoulders a good stretch, and should therefore be included in your regular yoga sessions.

Begin as for the rabbit, by sitting on your heels. Now

*The dog*

lean forward, your chest resting on your thighs and stretch your arms out in front of you, palms facing down. You should be able to feel the stretch in your lower back. Keep your head down too, so that the downward slope of your back and arms is uninterrupted. Take a deep breath and, as you exhale, lean forward onto your hands, lifting your buttocks up from your heels. You are now in the cat position, but rather than arch your back from here, bring your back up, buttocks first, until your legs are straight and your feet flat on the ground. For some this leg stretch will be enough, but if you are comfortable, being to 'walk' your feet without lifting your toes from the ground. Keep your head tucked in so that you are facing your feet. You will be able to feel your calve and ankle muscles at work. After a short period, bend your legs and return to the sitting position. Tuck your head down into your knees, let your arms relax and enjoy a quiet moment of rest.

*The boat (4)*
This is almost an inversion of the canoe and would work well with it as it contracts the muscles that the canoe stretches and vice versa. Although it looks as though it requires a great deal of muscular ability, it is in fact more of a balancing act than a feat of strength.

To begin, lie flat on your back with your arms by your side and your feet together. Take a deep breath and, as you inhale, lift your legs up into the air. They should be at a 45-degree angle to the floor. Inevitably this is going to feel very tiring, so now comes the balancing part. Stretch your arms our in front of you, rather like the arms-out pose adopted by the mummy in Hammer horror films, and then, keeping it

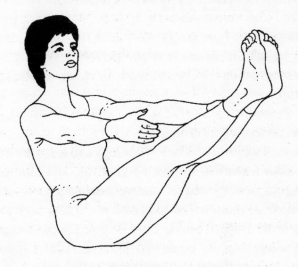

*The boat*

straight, lift up your torso till it too is at roughly a 45-degree angle to the floor. Your arms, legs and upper body should now form the shape of an upturned capital 'A'. Try to keep your facial muscles soft and avoid putting too much strain on your neck. To relax, on the exhale lower first your torso, keeping your arms outstretched to take some of the strain. Then lower your legs till you are in the lying down position once again. Repeat three times.

Balancing is a great way of switching off from the world as it requires intense concentration. Performance artists often find that, when performing a 'living statue' act, where they must remain motionless for sometimes up to hours at a time, a feat that requires 100 per cent balance in order to retain the effect of stillness, they become intensely aware of the world around them. When you first perform a balancing yoga posture you will be amazed by the richness of sound and sensation around you. You will also become conscious of how rarely we, as adults, simply relax in order to take it all in. It is the perfect way to gain a new perspective on life, but be warned, it can also be very, very tiring.

### The peacock (mayurasana)

This balancing act, where your legs and torso are supported by your forearms, just as the giant fan and long body of a peacock is supported on relatively delicate-looking legs, has an eerie, levitation look to it. And yes, it is as hard as it looks, so for the super-flexible only. If you are comfortable with the wheel then this could be within your grasp. If not, it may need the assistance and advice of a teacher.

Begin by kneeling with your knees spread apart. Your hands should be together, palms downward on the floor, with your

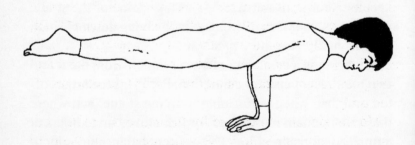

*The peacock*

wrists facing forward, in the space between your knees. Bend your elbows so that your upper arms, forearms and the floor form three sides of a square. Now lean onto your upper arms and feel your weight centre on your elbows. Only when you feel confident should you begin, on the exhale of breath, to straighten and raise your legs till they are supported by the central axis. Your body should now be parallel to the floor like an undisturbed seesaw. While you are balanced take short breaths but do not hold this position for more than a minute. To relax, breath in, and on the exhale allow your legs to bend and slowly meet the floor. Your weight should shift from the centre slowly, not abruptly.

*The fixed spot*

Concentrating on a fixed spot in your visual field is a time-honoured method for maintaining balance and equilibrium. Ballet-dancers, when performing series of pirouettes, prevent dizziness and disorientation by focusing their gaze on a fixed spot, at eye level, which their eyes seek out at every revolution. This punctuation in the spinning motion is virtually imperceptible to the onlooker, but if you watch closely you will notice that a dancer's head does not rotate at the same speed as the rest of the body. Rather, it will remain facing forward until the body is nearly at the half-revolution stage and then whirl round to the forward facing position once again, at a greater speed than the rest of the body.

Motion sickness is caused by the sense of balance becoming confused. Sailors advocate focusing on the only fixed point observable on a moving ship: the horizon. Similarly, the driver of a car is never the one who suffers from carsickness. This is because his eyes are fixed on the road.

### The eagle (12)

This is a gently balancing posture. Begin in the tadasana
and focus your gaze on a fixed
spot in front of you to help
maintain balance. Extend
your arms to either side so that
they are in alignment, and
then bring your left hand in,
palm facing, so that your fingertips touch your chin and
your wrist rests on the centre
of your breastbone. Now bend
your knees and bring the right
leg around the left so that your
right foot can curl in behind
your left ankle. If this seems
tricky try bending your knees
a little as this move will give
you additional flexibility.
Your legs should now be in
the position of a small child
miming that they need to go
to the toilet! However, you
should not bend over, but
keep your spine very straight.
Take your extended right arm,
bend it at the elbow and slide

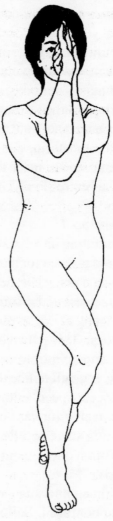

*The eagle*

it under your left elbow. Now curl your right hand round the your left hand so that palms are facing each other, though the left palm will be higher up than the right. Relax your shoulders and feel your chest muscles expand. Hold for a short period, concentrating on that fixed spot, before slowly uncurling, arms first. Repeat this movement for the other side.

This asana is very effective for promoting the elasticity of many muscle groups. Many people find that as their physical agility increases so too does their mental agility. So, if you are struggling with an emotional or intellectual problem and feel that your mind is too clouded try practising the eagle. It may help to free up your mind so that you see things more clearly.

*The scissors (6)*
This asana is so called because it mimics the action of a pair of scissors, where the handle moves in diametric opposition to the blade. If you follow the instructions carefully you will feel an enormous benefit in your lower back as well as in your shoulders and neck. Begin by lying on your back in a crucifix pose, with your feet together. Consciously make yourself relax and, taking a deep inward breath, lift your right leg into the air. Think of your leg as stretching lengthwise as well as upwards.

Once your leg is at right angles to the floor, exhale and bring your foot down to rest on the floor to the left of your body, keeping both legs stretched out straight. Your right hip will rise from the floor but keep your arms and shoulders firmly planted. To assist this movement, turn your head to the right, just as the handle of a pair of scissors would

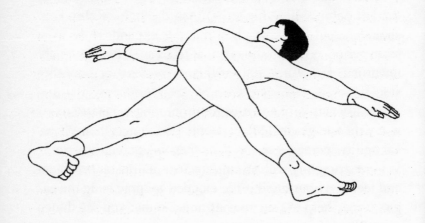

*The scissors*

move with the action of the corresponding blade. Relax and hold this posture for at least two minutes. Try taking another breath and stretching your right leg a fraction further. However, do not jerk – you are not scoring the winning goal for your country. To come out of this position, raise your right leg to the 90-degree angle and slowly lower it to the floor. Repeat for the other side.

This movement is often incorporated into aerobic workouts as a way of toning the inner thighs. However, the object here is not to flash from one side to the other, but to luxuriate in the stretch. Your thighs will tone up naturally without recourse to such frantic exercise.

### The twist (10)
This looks like a halfhearted version of the previous exer-

cise but actually requires an equal dose of concentration and will give your calves and ankles a good stretch too. Lie on your back in the crucifix pose as before, with your feet together and your toes pointing upwards. Take your right heel and lift it so that it rests on top of your left toes. Resist the impulse to raise your head and try to keep your neck and facial muscles soft. Now, upon the exhale, turn your feet so that they point, still one on top of the other, towards the left. As in the scissors posture, turn your head to face in the opposite direction, keeping your arms and shoulders to the floor. Your hips will naturally follow your leg movement. Hold this pose for a minute or two, then point your feet straight upwards once more, and return your right leg to its original position. Repeat the movement to the right, your left foot on top this time, and your head

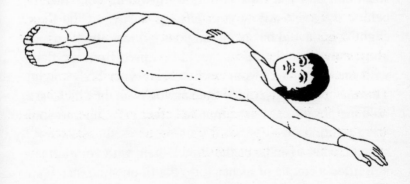

*The twist*

facing left. Repeat three times for each side bur remember to hold the pose each time.

For a bigger stretch, lift both legs in the air, feet together, and twist them down to the right until your knees touch the floor and your thighs are at right angles to the body. You will feel the whole of your spine expand, but remember to keep your shoulders on the floor and your head facing in the opposite direction. Return slowly to the centre and repeat for the other side.

### The leg lift (11)

This is a good exercise for people who are trying to lose weight or feel that their stomach muscles have lost some of their tone. It is similar in essence to the stretching exercises performed by athletes limbering up for a training session, and it helps to stretch the hamstrings and is great for relieving, and indeed preventing, stiffness.

Begin by lying on your back with your feet together and your arms by your sides. Bring your right knee up to your chest and pull it a little closer by entwining your fingers behind the knee. Allow your left leg to rise off the floor slightly, but avoid balancing on your tailbone. In the upper body, only your shoulders should be raised from the floor with the majority of your back bearing your bodyweight. This may be as much of a stretch as you want, in which case hold the pose for at least a minute before relaxing into your lying position.

If you want to enhance the stretch then, with your left leg still lifted a couple of inches form the floor, straighten your right leg so that the foot is pointing above and beyond your head. Use both hands, clasped round the ankle, to maintain

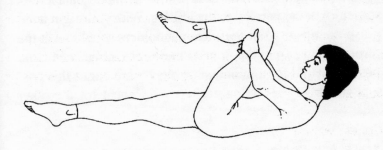

*The leg lift*

*The advanced leg lift*

this pose. Remember, of course, to keep your back firmly on the floor.

The truly rubber-limbed can move onto the advanced stage of this position. Use your left arm to maintain balance by stretching it out parallel to the left leg. With your right hand grasp the tips of your toes. Your shoulders should be at the same distance from the floor as they were in the knee-bend position. Hold for a minute, and then come out of this posture by slowly reversing each stage. Repeat for the other side.

### The sideways leg lift (9)
This posture is also referred to, rather confusingly, as the wheel. It stretches the leg and back muscles and requires as much balance as it does flexibility. Lie on your left side rest-

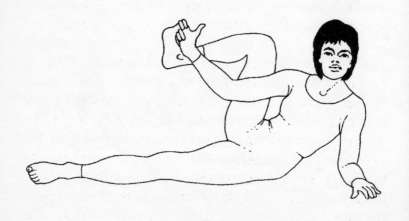

*The sideways leg lift*

ing your head on your left hand. Make sure that your are lying in a straight line and not bending at the waist or knees, or inclining forward. Find a spot, at eye level, on which to focus throughout this exercise, to maintain equilibrium. Once you achieve a stable position take your left forearm and lay it out flat in front of you. Bend your right leg up and towards your right ear, and grasp your toes with your right hand. Keep facing forward, gazing at your spot. Take a nice deep breath and, as you exhale, straighten your right leg, maintaining your hold of the toes. Your two legs should now form a right angle. Hold this pose and consciously relax your facial muscles.

This pose is said to represent the wheel of creativity and so should be serene. If your inclination is to frown, then try to smile; you will feel the muscles in your forehead and cheeks begin to relax, and your mood relax with them.

To come out of this pose, slowly bend your leg down and then lift it back onto the other leg. Now turn around slowly and repeat the movement for the other leg.

*The wide side-stretch (prasarita padottanasana) (19)*
This is a variant on the dog asana, and will give your back, hips and legs a powerful stretch. However, if you have back problems do not attempt the full stretch. If you are back problem-free, begin by sitting on your knees with your toes curled so that they are in contact with the floor and your heels are facing upwards (like an athletes' feet on the starting blocks). Place your hands, palm downward, in front of your knees, shoulders'-width apart. Leading with your buttocks, and keeping your head tucked down so that you face your feet, raise your back till your arms and legs are straight. Now

*The wide side-stretch*

There are two ways to come out of this posture. You can transfer the weight gently to your hands and allow your knees to bend down towards the floor. Alternatively, shuffle your feet towards the centre, till they are about one to two feet apart. Now shift the weight from your hands to your feet by compressing your abdomen into your back. Your body will naturally rise upwards with the assistance of the upper leg muscles. However, it is imperative that you keep your legs straight as bending the knees will deflect some of the strength away from your upper legs and prompt you to jerk yourself upwards to compensate.

If you suffer from any back problems, try doing this posture with a chair. From a standing position pace your feet around four feet apart and then slowly bend your upper body, from the hips, till they are at a right angle to the floor. Stretch out your arms and hold onto the chair. Remember to keep your weight centred on your feet and feel the stretch in your legs. Relax this hold by walking towards the chair so that you are supported as you move back into a standing position.

### The warrior (21)

This is a very empowering pose, reminiscent of the postures struck by ancient warriors about to commence battle. As you would expect, it is an excellent asana for promoting feelings of assertiveness and self-confidence. Begin in the tadasana and raise your arms to chest height, palms facing down, so that the tips of your fingers are touching. Your elbows should be extended straight out on either side. Now pace your feet apart to a distance of four feet and stretch your arms to their fullest extent. Ensure that your toes are pointing forward

*The warrior*

and your feet are flat on the floor. Your spine should be straight and your shoulders relaxed. Point your right foot out to the right and slowly bend your right knee to the side. Keep your left leg straight with the toes pointing forward. If you can, try to bend your right knee so that your thigh is at right angles with your lower leg. Take care not to let the right knee overshoot the lower leg as this puts pressure on the ankle and reduces the effectiveness of the stretch as well as jeopardising your balance.

Hold this pose for at least a minute and then return to the central stance. Repeat the movement for the other leg.

### The salute to the sun (surya namaskar)

As the name suggests, the 'salute to the sun' was created as a way of giving thanks for the dawn of another day. The series of movements that follow serve as an excellent warm-up to a yoga session as they rejuvenate and flex every muscle of the body. It can also be a complete session in itself as for every forward movement there is its backward complement, for every left-hand stretch a right-hand one, and so on. Some people base their regular yoga sessions on the Salute to the Sun, incorporating other asanas into the sequence.

It is very important to study and master each movement and to perfect the art of moving from one to the next with fluidity. An observer should believe that you are performing an unbroken ritual or dance rather than a series of stretches punctuated by awkward breaks. Breathe from your diaphragm as this will feed oxygen to every area of your body and keep your energy level constant.

Although these stances are quite safe, they should not be

done by pregnant women or those who are menstruating, unless under expert supervision. If you suffer from hypertension (high blood pressure), a hernia, clots in the blood or pain in the lower back, they are not recommended unless on the advice of your doctor. Most doctors will approve of yoga as a form of exercise, especially if you consult a teacher to keep you right, but it is best to check.

1   Begin by facing East, the direction of the rising sun. Even if this means facing a blank wall, try to fill your mind with the image of the sun just beginning to appear over the horizon. Even if it is the end of a busy day, concentrate on that beautifully still, expectant moment just before the sky begins to lighten. Stand up straight in the tadasana, with your feet together. Place your hands, palms together, at chest level, in the praying posture.

2   Take a deep breath and, as you inhale, stretch your arms up as far as you can without taking your feet

off the ground. Lean backwards, pushing out your
pelvis a little, with your
palms facing the ceiling.
Allow your head to tilt
backwards so that you are
looking up at your hands.
This is a glorious, celebra-
tory posture. Imagine you
are hailing the first rays of
sun and that the sky is
streaked with early morn-
ing gold and blue.

3  Take another deep breath
and, as you exhale, lower
your arms and bend your
upper body at the hips, not
the waist, and lower it
towards the ground.
Lower your head too, so
that it follows the line of
your back and arms. Keep
your feet flat on the
ground and try to reach
your ankles or even the
floor at your feet with
your fingertips or palms.
Do not force this: if you
cannot reach the floor, let
your hands hold onto the

lowest part of the legs they can reach. Don't be disheartened if this is only the knees, as the next time this imaginary sun rises you will be able to stretch a little further.

4    On an inhale, bend both your knees and lift your head so that you face upwards and forwards.  Place your hands on either side of your feet to support you. Now gently push your right leg backwards in a long, lunging movement, until your right knee touches the ground. Curl your right toes under so that they touch the floor and your heel faces upwards and relax your shoulders. Hold for a breath and then bring your right leg back to the knees-bent position and repeat the movement for your left leg. Do these movements gently, remember you are perform-

ing a smoothly flowing dance, not violent leg-lunges in an SAS training camp.

5   Keep both hands on the ground, palms down, and raise the head slightly. Lift your hips a little and incline them slightly forward. Taking a deep breath, stretch both legs out together backwards. You can either slide them or step backwards, but don't be tempted to do a big leap unless you are used to lunges, as this can put an unpleasant strain on your upper body. Now raise your body off the ground, supported by your straightened arms, so that your head, back and legs are in alignment. Think of the first of the sun's warmth touching the crown of your head, and feel the world waking up around you, just as every part of your body

is waking up and becoming energised.

6   Take a couple of deep breaths of fresh morning air, and on an exhale, push your knees into the floor and slightly raise your buttocks, so that your stomach and abdomen are not in contact with the floor. Bend your elbows a little further and bring your chest and chin to the floor. Continue the out-breath and lower your whole body, apart from your stomach and abdomen into the floor, straightening your legs and keeping your toes curled under. Your body is now being supported by the hands at shoulder level and also by the toes. Hold this pose as you take a few deep breaths.

7   On an inhale, straighten your arms so that your

back hollows and your chest curves out the way. Tilt your head backwards, facing the sun as it rises into the sky. Your stomach and abdomen will now be in contact with the floor, but keep your toes curled under so that your legs get a good stretch. Hold this pose for a minute and imagine the feel of the sun on your face. You should now be in the cobra position, which is that of a snake rearing up to strike.

8   Take another deep breath and push your whole body upwards, leading with the buttocks. Keep going until your arms and legs are straight and tuck your head in so that you face your feet. You should now be in an inverted V position. Make sure that your bodyweight is distributed evenly between the curled under toes of your feet and the palms of your hands.

Take a deep breath and feel the muscles of your legs and arms come to life.

9   Upon an exhale, push the hips slightly forward and lunge forward with the right leg so that it comes to rest with the knee bent and the right foot flat down between your hands. Remember to do this slowly, even though it is very tempting to make the movement quickly.

10  Breathe in and as you exhale, straighten the right leg, bending the upper body forward and down from the hips. Now bring your left leg in so that it stands beside your right. Lift your buttocks high and try to touch your toes, keeping your head tucked down.

11  Inhale and slowly lift the spine, visualizing it as unrolling your vertebrae one at a time. Raise your arms

above your head with the
palms facing the ceiling,
and lift your head so that
you are facing directly
into the risen sun. Allow
yourself to lean back a little into the stretch, but
keep your feet firmly
planted on the ground.

12 Lower your arms to your
sides and straighten your
legs and spine. Keep your
head erect and bring the
palms of your hands to-
gether at chest level. You
have now returned to the
praying position with
which you began and your
body should be singing
with energy and the sun in
your mind's eye blazing
with warmth.

Salute the sun six times at first, gradually increasing the
number of repetitions until you are comfortably doing the
routine 24 times. Of course, if you happen to be tired on a
certain day, do not force yourself to do so many. Yoga is not
about hard and fast rules; the way you feel and your enthusiasm for your practice is much more important than notching
up 24 sun salutes a day.

## Inverted postures

Inverted postures will initially seem very strange. After all, few of us have done a decent shoulder stand since we were in single figures and are quite unaccustomed to finding ourselves upside down. However, according to ancient yogic wisdom, a child's predilection for upending itself is a healthy instinct as it gives the blood circulation a wonderful boost and help you to feel really in touch with your body. Consider how good it feels, after an exhausting day, to take off your shoes, put your feet up and feel the fatigue drain from your legs. Turning yourself upside down is really just an extension of this.

Please note that these are not suitable exercise for pregnant or menstruating women, or for those suffering from arthritis in the back, shoulders or neck.

### The shoulder stand (sarvangasana) (8)

For this posture ensure that your back and neck are protected with a mat or folded blanket, even on a carpeted floor. You might want to give your shoulders the added support of a folded up blanket, as your weight will be resting on this part of your body.

Begin by lying on your back with your arms by your sides, with your palms flat on the floor. Bend your knees and lift them up towards your abdomen. As your lower back begins to lift off the floor, support it with both hands, and lift your knees to chest height. Take a deep breath and as you exhale straighten your legs and body so that they form a right angle with the floor. Avoid lunging by consciously transferring your weight to your shoulders. Your neck should not be taking the weight. Once you have achieved this pose, relax. Breathe normally and enjoy the sensation of your legs and feet being in the air. When you are ready to come down, slowly unroll your body onto the floor, laying your arms out flat to support your weight as it transfers from your shoulders.

Pay particular attention to your breathing pattern throughout this exercise. If you find that your breath is quick and shallow then you are tense. Such light breathing starves the muscles of oxygen and is therefore making the exercise counterproductive. If you are tense, abandon this posture meantime and attempt it again when you feel more confident.

When performed correctly, the shoulder stand takes pressure off the heart and stimulates whole body circulation. The fact that your chin is pressed into the chest is good for the thyroid, stimulating it and helping to iron out problems such as over- or under-activity, thereby helping to even out thyroid-based weight fluctuations.

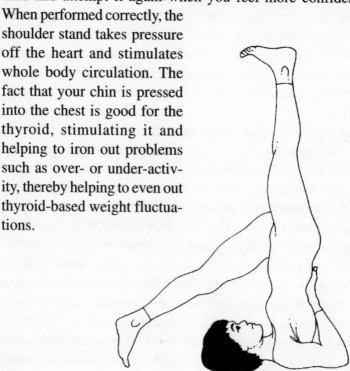

*The shoulder stand*

Once you have mastered the shoulder stand you may want to attempt it without the back support. To do so, repeat the previous instructions but allow your arms to rest lightly on the floor behind you. Remember that your legs and body should form a straight line, like a candle, which is another name for this asana.

Alternatively, you can try resuming the back support (splaying your fingers will broaden the support base) and bending your upraised legs so that the soles of the feet come together.

*The plough (halasana)*
This asana is so called because it resembles the shape of an old-fashioned Indian plough. It is also sometimes referred to as the wheelbarrow. Begin by lying on your back as before. Supporting the small of your back with both hands, bring your legs up over your head, keeping them as straight as possible. Continue lifting your legs up and over your head until the toes come to rest on the floor behind your head. Only when you are quite comfortable in this pose should you release the hold on your back and place your arms flat on the floor. Initially do not hold this pose for long, perhaps for ten seconds maximum. Once your body becomes accustomed to the plough you may want to hold it for longer.

An extension of the plough is the so-called 'choking position'. Obviously, if it makes you feel as if you are actually choking then stop at once. The name derives from the fact that the posture involves your thighs bracing your chin, and looks, to the uninitiated observer, as if you are engaged in a bout of self-throttling.

To achieve this unique pose, move into the plough as be-

*The plough*

fore. Now take a nice deep breath and, as you exhale, bend your legs, bringing your knees down to the floor so that they are as close to your shoulders as possible. Hug the backs of your knees with your arms and gently hold this position. Allow yourself to breathe naturally. To come out of this pose, return slowly to the plough before unrolling back onto the floor. Though at first this will seem like a strange contortion, it will come to feel very soothing and rejuvenating.

### The tripod

This rather tricky-looking posture is actually quite simple. It is just a question of confidence and following instructions precisely. If you are unsure, or find it too problematic, then this may be an asana to take to a teacher. Before you begin, take steps to protect your spine and neck by placing a blanket or mat underneath you, even if the floor is already carpeted.

Begin by standing on your hands and knees with the backs of your feet flat on the floor and your head and spine in alignment. Face downwards, and have your hands and knees placed shoulders'-width apart. Now place the crown of your head on the floor the same distance from each hand as the hands are themselves apart. These three points, the hands and head, must form the three points of an equilateral triangle, otherwise the posture will be imbalanced. Now bend your elbows so that the upper arms are at right angles to the floor. It is important that your weight is evenly distributed between the right hand, left hand and head as they are about to take the full weight of the body.

Carefully and slowly place your right knee onto your right elbow, making sure it is centred properly so that it does not slip. If this feels secure, place your left knee on your left elbow and balance. Caution is essential as you will end up performing a rather perfunctory forward roll if you do not achieve sufficient balance. Once you master this position, it is surprisingly comfortable. Concentrate

*The tripod*

on relaxed breathing. If you find yourself tensing and taking quick, shallow breaths, come out of this posture by lowering each knee in turn and slowly uncurling your torso, head and neck.

### The corpse posture (shavasana)

This is the ultimate in relaxation techniques and is an ideal way of cooling down after a yoga session. Begin by lying on your back. Ensure that you are neither too hot nor too cold and that you are as comfortable as you can be. Now visualise yourself lying on a warm beach. Take a deep breath and feel the sun on your face and let your muscles relax into the soft sand. Allow yourself to breathe normally and enjoy the moment. When you are ready, bring your mind's focus down to your toes. Give them a little wiggle and then flex them. As they relax you will feel a great release of tension. Now move to the soles of your feet and flex and relax them as you did for your toes. Let your heels be heavy in the sand. Remember not to strain, and to perform the exercise slowly. Move up through your legs, tensing and relaxing your knees and then your buttocks. Take your internal gaze to your hands and move up your arms to your shoulders. Lift and flex your shoulders a couple of inches from the ground, and then sink back slowly as you relax. Tense and relax your facial muscles then allow them to soften. Continue to breathe normally and give yourself up to this posture for at least five minutes, though you may find that you are enjoying it so much you want to hold it for longer. Give yourself a few moments to come out of this posture by focusing on where you are before you open your eyes.

## Advanced sitting positions

The most famous yoga pose of all is the lotus position; the cross-legged pose where each foot rests on the corresponding thigh. This is the pose the Bhudda is seen in as he sits down to meditate and is the greatest pose for clearing the mind in preparation for contemplation.

Anyone who has attempted this posture without any prior yoga practice will know only too well that it is a lot harder than it looks, and is one of the prime reasons why yoga tends to be unfairly written off as a weird enthusiasm for tying oneself in knots. However, if the very thought of the lotus makes your legs feel tired, don't worry. There are simpler yoga sitting positions.

*The thunderbolt (vajrasana) (13)*

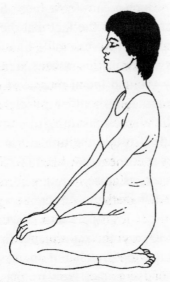

*The thunderbolt*

This is the most basic sitting position, and is described at the beginning of this chapter. It is an excellent posture for breathing exercises, as well as for improving digestion and toning the thighs and spine. It is also surprisingly absorbing as it requires concentration to keep the spine and head erect and resist the impulse to slouch backwards. Sitting too erect is also damaging as in so doing, you contract the lower back thus making the spine feel stiff, resulting in its becoming less flexible. Interestingly this is the sitting pose adopted by the Japanese for the tea ceremonies which can last up to five hours, which just goes to show how comfortable and beneficial this can be.

## The cow-face

Variations on the thunderbolt include the cow posture, or gomukhanasana, which means 'cow-face'. Some people say that the name derives from the fact that the accompanying eye exercises make the face resemble that of a cow rolling its eyes in distress! Despite this rather sad little thought, this asana gives your eye and facial muscles a gentle workout and stretches the arm and shoulder muscles.

Sitting in the thunderbolt posture, lift your right arm over your right shoulder, so that the upper arm is pointing upwards and the lower arm downwards. Place your hand, palm down, on your back, as close to that central bit where you can never quite reach with the sun-cream as possible. Take your left arm and bend it, upper arm down, lower arm up, round your back to meet the right hand. Clasp your fingertips together and feel the stretch, but do not strain your arms by pulling your hands together. Now for that facial. Keeping your head pointing forward, imagine a giant clock (and not a digital one!) in front of your face. Look at the number twelve, which should be above your natural line of vision, without tilting your head upwards or furrowing your brow. Your eye muscles should be doing all the work here. Think of those paintings in haunted house movies where the eyes move but the rest of the face remains motionless; that is the effect you are trying to achieve here. Now move your eyes down and out slightly to one o'clock, then two o'clock and so on until you arrive back at twelve. Hold each clock position for a second (count 'one elephant' each time), and continue to breathe normally. When you reach twelve, go round the clock again, but this time in an anticlockwise direction. When you reach twelve again, close your eyes and gently release your arms bringing them round to rest on your knees.

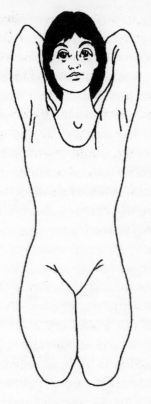

*The cow-face*

If your eyes feel strained, rub the palms of your hands together to make them warm, and gently cup one over each closed eye. Take a few deep breaths and relax. This eye exercise can be performed at any time and the warm-hand cupping is very effective for reviving eyes that have spent too long straining over text or staring at a VDU screen. It is also wonderfully rejuvenating when your eyes feel tired and gritty.

Learning to move our eyes independently of our heads not only strengthens eye muscles, it gives the neck muscles a rest too. An ophthalmologist called W. H. Bates believed that learning to use our eyes correctly, using the Bates Method, could even make the need for corrective lenses unnecessary. Whether this is so or not, the clock exercise above will certainly develop your awareness of your peripheral vision and help to improve your sense of balance. This latter is because, if we habitually turn our body to look, we risk throwing ourselves off the central axis of our stance; learning to look without moving unnecessarily can prevent this.

### The lion

This odd-looking asana is excellent for releasing neck and jaw tension, as well as being rather good fun. Sitting in the thunderbolt, take a deep breath and, as you exhale, stick out your tongue as far as it will go without straining, open your eyes wide and tense the neck and facial muscles.

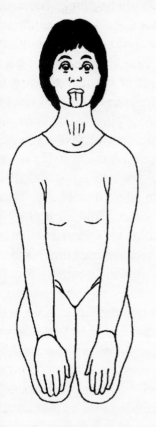

*The lion*

Brace your arms which should be straight with your hands on your knees. Hold this posture for the entire exhalation and then relax, remembering of course, to bring your tongue back in.

### The Egyptian

If the thunderbolt is not at all comfortable, and you are sure that this is not down to following the instructions incorrectly, try the Egyptian posture. For this you need a firm chair with an upright back, and of sufficient height to allow your feet to be flat on the floor with your lower legs at right angles to your thighs. Think of the ancient Egyptian statues of kings and queens; they are serene and perfectly poised. This posture is identical. Keep your back and head erect; your chin should not jut out further than your forehead, and your abdomen should be long and straight, not squashed. Like the thunderbolt position, this will become enormously com-

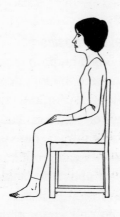

*The Egyptian*

fortable and, after a while, it will come to affect the way you sit outwith your yoga sessions – which is good news for the health of your spine as well as your posture.

Take care when getting in and out of this position. All too often, when we sit down on a chair we fall into it, rather than lower ourselves slowly downwards. The result of the former habit is that we make contact with the chair too heavily, sometimes causing jarring, and, when it is time to get up, we do the opposite, and swing up from the seat, causing uneven and unnecessary strain throughout the whole body. A good way of changing your habits is to practise sitting on an imaginary chair. Notice how you lower yourself down gradually when you know that there is nothing to break your fall, and how you gently tilt your back forward from the hips, keeping it in alignment with the head. As you raise yourself up again, note how your gradually straighten your whole body, legs, head and spine working in harmony. Now try this with a real chair.

### Easy posture or the tailor's position
If sitting cross-legged holds no problems for you, then it is simple to advance from here to more demanding yoga postures. The basic cross-legged position, sometimes known as the tailor's position and referred to as easy posture in Chapter 4, is actually quite a healthy posture providing you keep your back straight. Sit with each foot curled slightly under the opposite foreleg, just above the ankle. Straighten your back and place each hand, lightly, on the corresponding knee. Don't use your hands to pull you upright, and ensure that you are not leaning on your tailbone. Relax your knees and

*Easy posture or the tailor's position*

avoid jamming your feet under your legs thus causing the unpleasant sensation of 'pins and needles'.

### The butterfly
A progression from this cross-legged posture is the butterfly, which will stretch your inner thighs and your hips. This is especially good for anyone keen on horse-riding as it will stretch the muscles used to sit astride a horse's back, thus preventing saddle-soreness.

To achieve the butterfly move from the cross-legged position by stretching your legs out in front of you. Keep them straight, feet together, toes up, and make sure that you are not leaning back onto your tailbone by keeping your back and abdomen straight. Let your arms hang loosely by your sides with your palms on the floor. Now bend your knees away from the body and bring your feet together so that the soles are flat against each other. Cup your hands around your

*The butterfly*

feet. Concentrate on natural diaphragm breathing and, when you are relaxed, begin to move your knees up and down, like the wings of a butterfly. Keep the movement slow and even and repeat several times. For a final big stretch, gently push your knees down towards the floor. Hold and then relax, cupping your feet once again. When you can move your knees to the floor without using your hands and without difficulty, you are ready for the half-lotus.

### The half-lotus

Sit with your legs stretched out in front of you. Take the left ankle and bring the left foot so that the heel is against the groin, between the anus and vulva or scrotum, an area known as the perineum. Take your right foot and lift it across the left leg so that the toes are pointing into the back of the left knee and the heel is touching the groin. Keep your back straight; your weight should be centred on your pelvic floor and your knees touching the ground. Place each hand on the

*The half lotus*

corresponding knee with the palms facing upwards. This is a beautiful, symmetrical pose and you cannot but feel serene when in it. Let your facial muscles soften, close your eyes and hold.

To come out of it, bring your knees up slightly and release your feet, the right foot first. Stretch your legs out in front of you once more and take a deep breath before standing up. Always take your time coming out of these postures and vary the legs, leading with your right leg one time, your left leg the next.

*The lotus position (padmasana) (20)*
Named after the beautiful flower that symbolises perfection and creation, this is the ultimate sitting posture and should only be attempted by those thoroughly comfortable with the half-lotus. Many teachers, in fact, insist that this should only be taught on a one-to-one basis.

Begin by sitting on the floor with your legs stretched out, as

*The lotus position*

in the previous exercise. Take your right leg and lift it so the heel rests on the perineum, and the toe reaches high onto the left thigh. Bring the left foot across the right leg so that it rests high on the right thigh, the toes facing outwards, the heel pointing towards the groin. Again, rest both hands on the knees with the palms facing upwards. Hold this pose for a short time and remember, next time, lead with the other leg.

### The fish-lotus

From the lotus position you can move into this version of the fish asana, which is an entire body stretch but for the very gymnastic only. Sitting in the lotus position, take hold of each foot with the opposite hand, i.e. the left hand holds the right foot and vice versa. Take a deep, deep breath and, as you inhale, slowly hollow your back, arching it inwards, until the crown of your head comes to rest on the floor behind you. Do not roll backwards with your spine arched out-

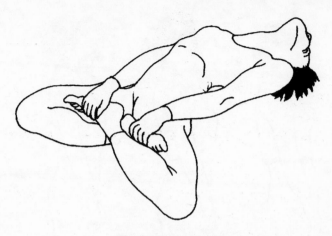

*The fish-lotus position*

wards as you will be forced to release your knees and feet abruptly in order to go with the roll! Relax the chest and shoulders and keep your knees firmly pressed to the floor.

When coming out of this posture take extra care not to jerk upwards or strain your shoulders and abdomen.

## The importance of posture

Good posture is much more than learning to walk nicely. In fact, it is the key to using our whole bodies correctly, enabling them to function properly and fight disease. This was discovered over a century ago by a young Australian actor called F. M. Alexander, who, when attempting to find the solution to a recurrent voice problem, discovered that he was not just misusing his vocal chords, but his whole body. The technique that he developed to correct this misuse, the Alexander Technique, is not a million miles away from the teachings and methods of yoga.

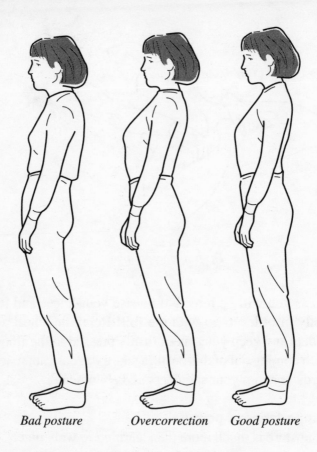

*Bad posture*    *Overcorrection*    *Good posture*

Alexander found that poor use of the body was not inherent, but learned. The proof of this can be found by observing the movements and postures of infants. For instance, a baby will sit upright if placed on the floor; its spine supple and erect, not curved backwards towards the floor. An unselfconscious infant will bend its knees, keeping its back straight, when lifting a heavy object, and sit and stand upright rather than slouch. So what happens to us that by the time we reach

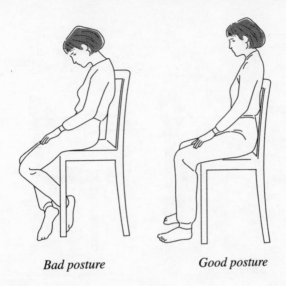

*Bad posture*          *Good posture*

adulthood we have developed a whole host of bad habits that bring about the aches and pains that inevitably make us feel even less inclined to move correctly?

Alexander believed that this is partly brought about by mimicking others. Children are often to be seen studying the movements and attitudes of parents and adults. It is a natural part of a child's learning process, and therefore, if they see their father bending stiffly down to lift a box of books, they will copy that movement. Even as adults we do something similar, unconsciously mimicking the gestures and attitude of someone towards whom we feel sympathetic. This is referred to as mirroring body language, and is a sure sign that someone is listening to you.

Another factor in the development of bad habits is enforced sitting for long periods of time, which we all endured for years at school, leading to all that craning forward and slouch-

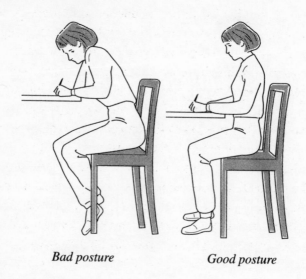

*Bad posture*          *Good posture*

ing back. Combine this with teenage awkwardness about a developing body and you have a recipe for disaster. Even breaks for PE and playtime fail to rectify this, as much organised sporting activity involves repetitive movements and fails to take into account the need for warming-up, cross-training and relaxation.

Finally, emotional and physical problems can contribute to poor posture. For instance, when we are depressed or sad, we let our shoulders droop and our spine sag. Consider the couple depicted by Picasso in his painting *The Tragedy*, dated 1903. Looking at this sombre work we can see, by the deep blue colours and forlorn expressions, that the couple have suffered a terrible loss or are enduring some appalling crisis. The emotional content is reinforced by their postures; stooped shoulders, arms twisted together, spines curved. Standing beside them is a child, presumably their son, who can be seen copying his father's hunched shoulders' pose.

Physical injury can also throw out our balance, causing us to limp or walk with a bent back, for instance. However, we often tend to continue limping long after it is necessary. We do not do this because we crave extra sympathy but simply because it becomes habitual. Many old people walk in such a way so as to 'compensate' for an old injury that may no longer even be noticeable. This is partly out of a fear that a change in habit will bring about the return of pain, though often the opposite is true. Luckily, as with yoga, there is no such age as 'too old' to begin learning the Alexander Technique. However, the younger you start the easier it will be, and the longer you will have to savour the rewards.

## The spine
The spine is the most important bone in the body, influencing the function and health of the nervous system, muscles and internal organs. Yet, for all its importance, we neglect it. Sportspeople and fitness enthusiasts pay enormous attention to their legs, arms, upper body strength, or whatever part of them they think is most important to achieving their ambitions. Far too few truly appreciate the workings and needs of the spine, without which the rest of their endeavours would be pointless. The fact that the spine still manages to retain its strength and flexibility at all when it is neglected is testament of how truly resilient it is.

Allowing the spine to stretch properly and regularly is one of the biggest favours you can do for your body. It will help to keep the vertebrae, and the discs between them, in alignment. Anyone who has ever suffered a slipped disc will tell you just how excruciating the results of poor alignment can be. Not only can it lead to injury, the resultant backaches and discomfort can seriously impinge on your quality of life, as well as your self-confidence.

Each disc has a semi-fluid centre, protected by an outer shell. Think of the vertebrae as individual building blocks, each with a cushion (disc) between them. If the blocks are pushed out of alignment so that they bear down heavily on one or other side of the cushion, the fabric of the cushion will wear away, and the stuffing (semi-fluid centre) begin to squeeze out. The attendant nerves are then subject to pressure, causing pain. Proper stretching exercises keep the vertebrae in their rightful place, thus giving damaged tissue the opportunity to repair itself, and preventing further damage.

# Chapter 14

# The Chakras

## Chakras

Some schools of yoga, believe that there are centres of psychic energy, known as chakras, placed in the sushumna, the central canal of the astral body roughly corresponding to the spinal column in the physical body. The chakras sit at various points between the base of the spine and the top of the head. Two schools of yoga, tantric and kundalini, practise meditation on each of them in turn.

Each chakra has its own yantra and its own mantra (apart from the topmost one). Starting with the lowest of them, the muladhara, situated between the anus and genitals, the meditator visualises its yantra while repeating its mantra, either inwardly or aloud, until ready to move on.

As the meditation works its way through the chakras, the latent energy of each one is released, imbuing the meditator with stronger and stronger sensations of warmth and light at the centre until, when the final meditation is completed, the physical will have merged with the spiritual – the meditator's consciousness merges with the universe.

The word chakra is a Hindu word meaning 'nerve centre' or 'wheel'. Each chakra has an individual 'character' and corresponds to a certain colour, element, mood and activity, as well as having a unique function in promoting bodily health. Additionally, each chakra is adorned with its own number of lotus petals, governed by the number of the body channels that conjoin at that point in the astral body. The positions of the chakras correspond to plexuses in the body, and to the acupuncture charts of traditional Chinese medicine. It is possible that there was the equivalent of chakras in ancient Western philosophy as the nature of each seems well suited. For example, the anahata chakra, which governs emotions, is situated near the heart – the internal organ to which we ascribe so much emotional feeling, describing ourselves as having a heavy heart, a fluttering heart, even a heart that is on fire!

The chakras are located where the namis, the carriers of Prana, the life force, cross. This is not unlike the belief that cosmic energy is sourced at the point where leylines cross, for instance, at Stonehenge. The chakras emanate energies that we need to live fulfilled lives, but unfortunately the channel by which these energies travel can become blocked, resulting in that feeling of being 'out of touch' with our body. Yoga exercises seek to unblock the flow of energy, and to allow you to tap into the kind of energy you need at a particular time. The chakras can be further encouraged to resonate by wearing the corresponding colour. If this latter seems a little unlikely, then consider how strongly colour can affect your mood, and how that can vary. One day orange is joyful and warm, the next garish. Green can be peaceful, or it can be insipid. Our fickleness could be down to the fact that we do not need, or perhaps even want, that kind of energy today.

Anyone wishing to practise this form of meditation needs

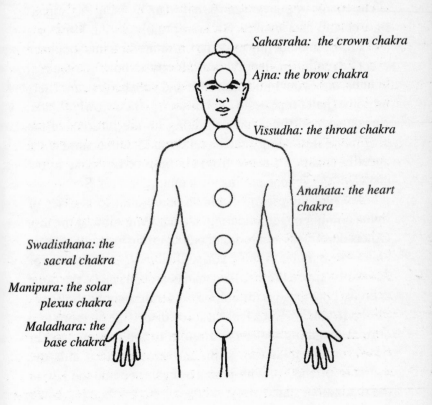

Sahasraha: the crown chakra

Ajna: the brow chakra

Vissudha: the throat chakra

Anahata: the heart chakra

Swadisthana: the sacral chakra

Manipura: the solar plexus chakra

Maladhara: the base chakra

*The seven major chakras*

detailed instruction from an experienced teacher over a long period of time, but the following exercise may give you just a flavour of the full effect.

The energy of a chakra can be called up by using the 'sound' of a chakra as a mantra. Sit comfortably, in the lotus or a variation, remembering to keep your spine straight, your head erect. Breathe in deeply, and slowly exhale for several breaths, until your mind feels clear and your body calm. Then, as you exhale, repeat the chakra sound, then slowly inhale. Repeat several times, concentrating on the location of the chakra, until its energy can be felt. You can concentrate on a specific chakra, or move from the base of the spine to the crown of the head, chanting each mantra in turn. Some people describe the effect of this as being akin to a series of lights coming on, culminating in a dazzling glow at the top. Others describe is as a series of bells, getting gradually higher and purer in note. In time, you will learn to sound the notes internally. If you prefer to see than hear, you can do the same exercise but visualise the colours rather than sound the notes.

Stop if you begin to feel dizzy or disoriented, return to a normal breathing pattern and return to the mantra another time. Initially chanting stills and soothes as it aids the sourcing of energy; with practice it can become the key to the meditative state.

## Maladhara

Found at the base of the spine, the perineum plexus, this chakra is close to the groin area. Despite this, it is not the chakra that promotes sexual energy, but rather strengthens attributes such as security and stability, and sharpens instinct. It is related to the element of earth. 'Mula' means root, and 'adhara' means support, so this is the chakra that gives us that grounded, content within ourselves feeling. If you find that you constantly seek reassurances from people, or rely on props like money, possessions or status to make you feel secure, this is the chakra you should be tapping into. It is also the chakra that will sharpen up your sense of smell. The colour red will stimulate this chakra, or chant the sound 'LAM' to call up its energy.

## Swadisthana

In Sanskrit, swadisthana means 'place of origin', and is located in the mid-abdomen at the prostatic plexus. This is the chakra that promotes sexual and sociable energy, making its colour, orange, ideal party wear. However, this energy can have negative connotations, such as jealousy or an overemphasis on the sexual side of relationships. Homing in on this chakra, either by visualisation or chanting its mantra, VAM, can help to keep this energy positive, and push tilted sexual emotions back into an upright position.

This chakra's element is water, and is the source of much creative energy. It is also related to the sense of taste.

## Manipura

Located in the solar plexus, the manipura, which means 'bright jewel of inner power', is the source of the 'fire in the belly' that propels us to great things. It is related to the element of fire and, according to ancient Chinese wisdom, is the centre of psychic power and the source of 'chi', which means 'life force'. By tapping into this chakra we are stoking the fire of our deepest power. Even conventional medicine cannot fault the logic of the Manipura; deep breathing, drawing oxygen into the region of the solar plexus, nourishes the organs of the abdomen, which are essential to good health. Take a deep, deep breath and feel your lower body respond.

The colour for this chakra is yellow, and its effect is akin to that of an antidepressant, without the side-effects. It boosts your inner confidence, but not by means of the ego, which is flattered by external agents only. If bright primary yellow is not your colour, try a darker, golden or ochre hue as these work just as well. Despite being such a happy colour (who doesn't respond to the yellow of buttercups or feel cheered by the glow of lamplight?) it is a colour we rarely wear. Could this be at the root of our famous Western lack of self-esteem?

The sound for this chakra is RAM, an appropriately thunderous note for such a superpower chakra.

## Anahata

This is the chakra that brings harmony to your emotions and the breath of life, which is very apt as it is located near the heart on the pulmonary plexus. Focusing on this centre can promote a sense of love for all living things, which will not only make you feel good, it will give your health a boost too. Think of the way that love can put a spring in your step, compared to the brooding, weighty feeling generated by hatred.

Green, also acknowledged by practitioners of colour therapy and Feng Shui as inducive to peace, is the colour for anahata harmony. It provides serenity and is perfect for a frenzied day of Christmas shopping or a highly charged day at the office. However, it is quite an emotional colour and is not advisable for situations where you may want to keep your feelings in check. Perhaps this is the reason green is considered unlucky at Christian weddings, lest it cause too many outbreaks of tears?

Anahata, which means 'self-sustaining' is related to the element air. Meditation upon this chakra involves focusing on the air that sustains life and that life sustains. Oxygen keeps us alive, we convert it into carbon dioxide, which keeps plants alive, who covert it back into oxygen; air is a never-ending cycle of life. The mantra for this chakra is YAM.

## Vissudha

Located at the branchial or pharyngeal plexus, this chakra is near the throat. It promotes steadiness and balance and is essential for keeping a level head. It is also the chakra of concentration and logic and its energy will induce fruitful study, whether you be about to embark on a diet of exams or wish to coolly weigh up the pros and cons of a new relationship or a new direction in life.

Wear blue to tap into Vissudha's energy, which will also help you to rid your mind of resentments and bones of contention, the very things which can block clear thought. It is also great for bending your mind round complex concepts. Its sound is HAM.

## Ajna

Naturally the head is related to the mind, but also to the spirit. Here the energies are not directed solely at earthbound needs and problems, but those of achieving oneness and spiritual reality.

The ajna is the 'third eye', set between your eyes at the

choroid plexus, which has control of all thoughts, whether incoming or outgoing. Its element is the mind, and it is considered, in yogic philosophy, to be the vertical eye of wisdom, as opposed to conventional, horizontal wisdom, and as such is related to the Divine. Our deepest insights, not just into the apparent world but that which is beyond it, derive from here. Wear or visualise indigo to stimulate your intuition and intellect, or chant the mantra OM in a shorter, lower tone than you will use for the next chakra.

The ajna is connected to the hypothalamus and pituitary glands, and its energy can be channelled towards regulating mind and body reactions, and ensuring that the messages your brain receives are not misleading.

## Sahasraha

This means 'a thousand petals' and is visualised as a thousand petalled lotus emanating from the crown of the head. In yogic texts it is symbolised as a thousand rays of light that create an effect similar to the halo of Christian symbolism. Located at the highest point of the body, it is fitting that sahasraha relates to the purest, most spiritual instincts of man. Its colour is white, the colour of angels and light, and meditation upon this centre produces that highly prized feeling of oneness with the universe. It is the link between the individual and the universal self and its mantra is the longer, higher sounding of OM.

## Warning!

The colours detailed above should not be seen as 'lucky' colours, or adhered to religiously according to mood: an orange dress will not transform you into a flirt! Avoid getting trapped in neurotic superstitions, such as blue for exams, as this will only make you unhappy. You will seek these colours naturally, in all probability you already do to some extent. It can help to visualise colours rather than wear them if you are inclined towards superstition. During a hectic day, visualise a field of green, or if you cannot get your mind straight about all those facts and figures, close your eyes and think of a boat, painted the colour of a summer sky.

## Kundalini

'Kundalini' means 'the coiled serpent' which is said to sleep at the base of the spine, where the muladhara chakra is located. Intense meditation can be used to awaken this serpent, which is sometimes described as being like a power cable, causing it to rise up through the chakras. It is said to release great psychic powers when it reaches the thousand-petalled lotus of the sahasraha chakra. Intriguingly enough, this practice is warned against as being too dangerous for the uninitiated. The yogics of old advise you strongly to seek the guidance of someone highly trained in the art of kundalini rather than attempt it alone.

# Chapter 15

# Ways to Unwind

## Vipassana (the witnessing meditation)

A witness sees events, verifies testimonies, mentally records what happens. One ceases to be a witness when one becomes involved, and, in court, a witness should never express their feelings on what they saw lest they mislead the jury by presenting a skewed version of the truth. To bear witness is both the easiest and hardest thing in the world to do. Easy to watch, but very hard not to interfere, to react or to judge.

Buddhists developed this meditation as a way of perfecting concentration and awareness and to gain an understanding of the impermanence of the universe. Change, they maintain, is inevitable and constant and, if we are to be happy, we must learn to accept it.

To do this meditation find something to witness: usually seating yourself at a window is best. The scene you witness need not be car-chase exciting. You could just as well witness someone mowing a lawn or children playing in the street. Take time to absorb yourself in what you are seeing. Be aware of any thoughts or reactions from within you, and rather than analyse them, observe them. Regard your reactions as part of this scene that you are witnessing. If you notice yourself judging what you are seeing, then add that too into the pot of the witnessed experience.

This is a very pure meditation, that brings the mind down to rest on one single purpose: to witness. It is not the same as going off into a daydream, as you are very aware of every nuance of the experience, from the breeze blowing through the window to the creak of a child's bicycle pedals. The feeling of at-oneness with what you see engenders a very powerful sense of inner peace.

## Prarthana (the surrender meditation)

This meditation is a great way of switching off. It is, literally, surrendering your thoughts and actions, and is extremely akin to what many of us did as teenagers after a hard day at school. However, unlike the experience of fraught teenagers, the object of this exercise is not to fret over feelings and thoughts, but to let them go.

Lie face downwards on the floor. You can use a mat, but not a pillow. Support your head with your hands, placed one over the other, palms down. Cross one foot over the other, at the sole not the ankle, and feel your weight pressing into the floor. If niggling thoughts persist, play a tape of restful music and let your mind become absorbed in it. You can take as long or as little a time over this as you wish, but you will feel very relaxed very quickly.

## Zen driving

Meditating whilst driving may not sound very safe, but in fact Zen driving is about as safe as you could get and your driving instructor would definitely approve! Practising this meditation behind the steering wheel is also a great antidote to road rage, that tightening of the chest and bubbling of the brain that comes with too many traffic jams and ill-mannered motorists scraping past you at the lights.

Driving Zen-style is very simple. You drive, you do all the things you should do when driving like checking the wing mirror, watching your speed, watching the road and the other motorists. But you do nothing else. Don't think about that meeting you should have been at ten minutes ago, or the fact that the children need to be picked up at four o'clock and when you are going to find time to go to the supermarket. Forget all that, because right now you are driving, you are at one with the car, the speedometer, the traffic lights, the van behind you.

As you can imagine, Zen driving is also a great way to recapture that sense of exhilaration and wonder that you had the day you drove a car by yourself for the first time. Which of course, is the spirit of Zen: taking the world as new every single moment.

# Chapter 16

# Grabbing the Moment Meditation

Once you gain experience in meditating, it is possible to go into meditative mode for short periods whenever you need to. All it takes to meditate in this way is a few seconds of concentrated focus, and you will find yourself refreshed and ready to cope with stress. We have used the right hand in some of the meditations described below: if you are left-handed, use the thumb and two fingers of the left hand instead.

### The wedding ring meditation

To meditate on your wedding ring, simply inhale deeply and bring the tip of the thumb on whichever hand you wear your wedding ring into contact with the first two fingers so that the ring finger is slightly raised.

As you exhale slowly, focus your eyes on the ring, gazing at a glint that catches the light. Repeat four or five times.

### The red light meditation

Next time you are held up at traffic lights, stare at the red light with both eyes, willing yourself into it. Breathe in and out slowly as many times as you can until the lights change, and you will take off in a better frame of mind than before.

## Meditation at work

Most people have jobs that involve doing the same thing day after day, be it something as active as waiting tables in a restaurant or as sedentary as working in an office in front of a computer. Most people at some time or other during their working day find themselves drifting off into their own thoughts: use this time to improve your work efficiency by meditating.

The moment you first realise you are lost in thought, visualise a blank screen and then picture yourself on that screen, seeing yourself work faster and more productively, more safely and more creatively, than you have ever worked before. Try to hold this image for a moment or two, and in time you should find yourself working more efficiently and getting more out of the job too.

## Spot meditation

Breathe in deeply and touch the tip of the first two fingers of your right hand with your right thumb. As you breathe out focus your attention on the first thing that catches your eyes and maintain the focus for four or five more breathing cycles.

## Pain relief meditation

If you suddenly feel pain, for instance if you stand up too quickly and find you have an agonising pain in the back, focus your thoughts on the part of the body that is aching. Again join the thumb and first two fingers of the right hand and breathe deeply taking the breath right into the pain. As you breathe out, see the pain being carried away on your expired breath.

## Countdown to calmness

For a brief meditation that brings instant calm, breathe in, once more touching the tip of the thumb with the tips of the first two fingers of the right hand. Breathe out slowly, counting down from ten to zero as you do so, visualising each number in turn in your mind's eye, watching one fade as it is replaced by the next. When you reach zero, you will be infused with a feeling of serenity you thought out of reach a few moments before.

## Back to the future

Find an old photograph of yourself and focus your attention on it. Project the image you are looking at forward to the present and try to see if the person is still you. Then let him or her fade back into the photograph. After the meditation try and work out if the boy or girl in the photograph would be happy with what he or she has become. If so, good for you: if not, by taking up meditation you have at least taken a step in the right direction.

# Chapter 17

# **Frequently Asked Questions**

### Is meditation selfish?

There will always be people who subscribe to the notion that anything a person does for themselves is selfish, be it spending money on a new outfit, or putting their feet up for ten minutes. Neither of these two things are selfish activities, and nor is meditation. In fact, meditation could almost be regarded as a selfless activity in that it benefits those around you as well as yourself.

Think about it. If you meditate regularly you become more attuned to your real self and learn to like yourself. This in turn makes you more amenable to other people. Also, as you become more sensitive to your own inner needs, so you respond more to the needs of others. You learn to focus on what you are doing, while you are doing it, and so become more efficient at work. In short, you become a kinder, more sensitive, more reliable person, and that is to the good of everybody, isn't it?

### I've followed all the meditation exercises and nothing happens. Does this mean I can't meditate?

No, it just means that you are expecting far too much from your meditations. When someone prays they do not expect God's voice to boom down from heaven in response, and neither should you expect dramatic, sudden changes.

Take your time, follow the exercises and even though it may sometimes feel as if nothing is happening, there will be profound changes going on at a deeper level. You may emerge from a meditation one day and discover that you are beginning to feel very different, and those around you will certainly notice the difference.

It could be that, by expecting too much, you are distracting yourself and thereby preventing yourself from meditating successfully.

### Will I have to change my lifestyle in order to feel the benefits of meditation?

No, but you very likely will change your lifestyle as you become more sensitive to your bodily needs and sensations. People who meditate regularly find that they gradually start shedding bad habits, like drinking or eating too much, because the stress levels, which prompted these behaviours in the first place, have significantly reduced. They also find that, once they have learned to listen to their bodies, they actively want to take better care of their health, and will endeavour to use less salt, less caffeine, give up smoking, and cut out red meat. Of course, healthy people do have better concentration, because they are not distracted by illness or discomfort, which will make the process of meditation much easier, and therefore more satisfying.

### Can meditation help with serious medical and emotional problems, or is it only for those that are healthy and 'nearly well'?

For serious emotional and mental problems, you should al-

ways seek the advice of a doctor or counsellor. This is because, when you meditate and discover your inner self, you
will inevitably unearth some things that will make you feel
very uncomfortable, even distressed, such as past deeds of
which you are ashamed and the remorse for which is deeply
embedded in your psyche, or tormenting feelings of self-
loathing. And when you meditate on these kinds of things,
they can quickly become unbearable. Even very stable people often require the help of a teacher to get them through
the difficult times. However, having said that, with care,
meditation can be very helpful, very comforting, and promote the positive feelings that heal.

Serious medical conditions cannot be 'cured' by meditation, but their symptoms can often be alleviated and their
cure hurried along by regular practice. Cancer patients, for
example, are often advised to consider meditation as a way
of dealing with pain, and, very importantly, learning to live
in the moment, rather than obsessing destructively on
thoughts of death. And although meditation is not yet being
prescribed as a way of combating disease, studies conducted
in America suggest that learning Transcendental Meditation
(TM) has been of enormous benefit to patients suffering from
ailments such as coronary artery disease, hypertension and
trait anxiety. In some cases, TM was not just effective as a
preventative or palliative, but also as a treatment.

## Can meditation help me sleep better?
Sleeplessness occurs for a variety of reasons. It could be
that our lifestyles are so erratic that our body clock is wildly
out of synch, and our body and brain cannot respond to an
artificial deadline for sleep. Or it could be caused by stress,

accumulated during the day, finally taking its toll: how can we expect to sleep if our mind is rattling through the minutes of the last meeting and constantly replaying that scene where you yelled at the kids for no real reason? Jet lag, alcohol, caffeine and late meals also play their part.

There are many ways to deal with sleeplessness, such as regulating the hours you sleep, drinking camomile tea or a hot milky drink, taking a warm bath and taking an hour to unwind before crawling between the sheets. Meditation is a method that will, in time, ensure that you do all these things quite naturally, and will also help to combat the stress overload that more and more of us are taking to bed. Meditation in the early evening, when the day's work is done, is particularly conducive to good sleep and will also help you to relax during your well-earned time off.

One last thing to remember: meditation is extremely invigorating and many find that their need for sleep is actually reduced with regular meditation.

### What if I forget to meditate for days at a time? Will the benefits be lost?

Like taking vitamin supplements or exercise, regularity will greatly increase the benefits of meditation. However, don't be discouraged if you forget or don't always feel like it, though it is always worth the effort trying to overcome the latter feeling. As you begin to feel the benefits of meditation in your everyday life, your motivation will increase.

# Chapter 18

# Ten Reasons To Start Meditating

1  You will increase your sense of self-worth, and learn to value yourself more. This will not only make you feel happier, but also help you to make better decisions, rather than allow yourself to be taken for granted, or bullyingly demand your own way.

2  You will feel better towards your fellow man. Being unforgiving and judgemental seems easy and effortless at the time, but in fact all negative emotions take their toll on your health and emotional wellbeing. Loving thy neighbour will relieve you of a lot of stress, and also open avenues of potential enjoyment for yourself. There are few things more delightful, and humbling, than finding a friend where you had convinced yourself you had an enemy.

3  Like the Taoists, you will learn to accept, rather than fear, change. Our lives are always in a state of flux: even very old people with paid off mortgages and grown-up children have to come to terms with the fact that there are still changes to come, including the greatest change of all, death. Resisting change is like trying to fit the cork back into a champagne bottle; it is pointless and uses up a lot of energy. Learning to swim with the tide will greatly enhance your sense of oneness with it all.

4   You will become more alert and responsive. Your boss will be delighted, as will your colleagues, when they notice how you have become the person who can remember where the files are, who will be attending the meeting, and who takes what in their coffee. They will also be enormously flattered that you have paid sufficient attention to remember!

5   With regular practice, you will be setting yourself up for a lifetime of improved health. Your stress levels will be significantly reduced, rendering you not only stouter of heart, but also with greater immunity to germs, deeper, healthier breathing patterns, clearer skin and eyes, and fewer wrinkles. Added to this is the fact that you will have less need of artificial stimulants to cope with stress, which will also benefit your health.

6   Greater sensitivity to your inner self will grant you greater control over your impulses. You will find that not only can you resist another drink, or another chocolate, but also another spree with the credit card, or another pointless sexual liaison. Quick 'mood fixes' will no longer appeal to you, because you will recognise them for what they are, and ultimately find that you do not need them.

7   A sense of meaning will be restored to your life. Religious meditators find that their spiritual life is greatly enriched by meditation, feeling that it has brought them closer to themselves and therefore to God. But even non-religious people reap spiritual dividends. The sense of oneness with the world that they develop often spurs them toward greater participation in the world, particularly in the voluntary, caring sector, which is a very rewarding and uplifting experience.

8   You become more sensitive to your own true needs, desires and feelings, and this enables you to be more sensitive to those of others. Thus you become a better friend, partner, child, and forge stronger, more fulfilled relationships.

9   Being more centred helps you to recognise and alter destructive behavioural patterns, such as overeating or overcompetitiveness. These patterns only serve to sap your energy and keep you in a rut. Meditation helps you to reclaim all those wasted resources.

10  Last, but not least, meditation will help to restore your sense of wonder. It will enable you, like a Zen Buddhist, to look at the world from one moment to the next and see it as if for the first time.

# Chapter 19

## Two Case Studies

### Mary

(Mary, 45, is divorced with one son, and took up meditation two years ago.)

Mary and Mark had barely spent any time together since their son left home in 1992 to go to university. In the spring of 1994, Mark confessed to having had an affair with a female colleague, though insisted it was over. Mary suggested they attend Marriage Guidance counselling, but Mark refused. In the summer of that year he announced his intention to leave the marital home and move in with his lover. He asked Mary for a divorce and she refused.

After Mark's prompt departure, Mary become obsessive in her desire to keep up appearances. Although she was actually feeling extremely anxious and vulnerable, she maintained an outward cheerfulness that fooled no one who knew her well, but somehow made them feel that they should keep their distance. Mary was known to be a very emotionally proud woman. During this time, she was also angry, felt that she hated Mark, and that she had wasted her life by being married to him. Even when her son came home to visit her, she felt that she could not really enjoy his presence. Added to her emotional distress was a physical one: for the first time in her life, Mary suffered from eczema, which began between her fingers, but gradually spread to the rest of her hands, making everyday tasks extremely uncomfortable.

Finally, she visited the doctor, who diagnosed depression and prescribed tranquillise rs, which Mary refused to take because her mother had been addicted to tranquillisers and she feared she would become so too. For her hands he prescribed cream and a course of antibiotics. Unusually, perhaps, for an older male doctor, Mary's GP also suggested she try 'an alternative therapy' and gave her a leaflet about meditation.

'I would have written it off as hippy rubbish if it hadn't been for the fact that a doctor had handed it to me, which is silly really isn't it, that his white coat made all the difference?' Desperate rather than interested, Mary attended a lecture and bought a couple of paperbacks outlining basic techniques. She was relieved to note that no one seemed to be preaching any kind of religion alongside the meditation. 'I went home and tried to do them all, about three times each, and by the end of the night I was so wound up I wanted to cry!'

However, in the cool light of morning, she read the books calmly and felt quietly inspired. At the forefront of her mind was the notion that meditation could help her to be at peace with the world 'because I felt that me and the world were at total odds, and I hated feeling that way. It made me feel ugly and unpleasant. I suppose my self-image must have been very poor.'

Having always been a very organised person, Mary set about her meditations in systematic fashion, sitting down to breathing exercises every morning. The exercise she found the most helpful was the metta-bhavana. 'It's such a beautiful meditation, and the very first time I did it I felt as if I had turned the clock back twenty years.' Friends and colleague began to notice the difference, especially as Mary was now beginning to open up and tell them what had happened, and even admitting how badly she had felt about it all. Her eczema began to clear up of its own accord (the cream and antibiotics had made no impact on the condition), though it does return when she is under stress. She realised that she had achieved something like a state of grace when she contacted Mark to tell him that she would, after all, grant him a divorce.

'I learned to like myself, and once I did that, I stopped being afraid of what people thought of me, and stopped being afraid of change.'

### Shakyafinha

Shakyafinha was ordained as a Buddhist in 1996, and, at 32, is the fourth youngest order member in the world.

In 1988, Shakyafinha was working as a civil servant in the west coast of Scotland. He didn't hate his job, or his family, or his friends, but he did feel dissatisfied and as if he was constantly on the lookout for something else. He was drawn to the idea of meditation because he wanted to understand himself more and better integrate with his world. At first he tried Christian meditation, but found he could not cope with Christian doctrine. But then he learnt about the teachings of the Buddha and realised he had found his direction. 'The Buddha, you see, is not a creator God. We revere him for what he represents and derive inspiration from his life. He achieved enlightenment 2,500 years ago, and I can achieve it too.'

Meditations included breathing exercises to achieve still-ness of the mind. 'Moving on to focus on the emotions was harder,' Shakyafinha recalls. 'Having positive emotions to-wards myself was a reversal of the usual trend, which I'm sure is the case for most people: we're only really used to criticising ourselves and others.'

The meditation he found most effective in combating this tendency was the metta-bhavana. 'You have to start from where you are and learn to cultivate a loving kindness. You can't expect to feel it straight away.' Now a teacher of medi-tation himself, Shakyafinha urges students not to try to force themselves into doing something they don't feel. It will come with time. As he continued to meditate he had a number of cathartic experiences, when he came across aspects of him-self that he had not previously been aware of. 'But I learnt that you cannot reject your self, or any parts of it. I had to work through it all and come out feeling good about myself or I wouldn't be able to properly feel good about others.'

Shakyafinha found himself increasingly drawn to the Bud-dhist way of life, and in 1989 decided to take a step back from it. He gave himself a year to think about it, and then decided that it was the life for him. In 1992 he gave up his job, and now works at a Buddhist centre, making full use of his administrative skills as well as teaching. Meditation is a central part of his life, and he meditates twice a day, begin-ning at 7.30 a.m. when he arrives at the centre.

'My parents don't really understand why I became a Bud-dhist, but they saw me become more myself and happier, so they accepted it. They saw the outer effects.' And the inner effects? 'I am much more content. I have found a meaning to my life.'

## Postscript

Once you have learned to meditate, it is a skill that you will have for the rest of your life, but while it will give you a sense of inner serenity it does not mean that you are free of pressures and disturbing emotions. Meditation is not an escape from these problems: it enables you to see them as something you can deal with.

Once you have become used to meditation, you will find you can practise it anywhere – on a train, in an aeroplane, at your office desk during the course of a working day.

And remember there is no right way to meditate and no wrong way to meditate. The only right way is the one that you are most comfortable with, the one that enables you to get out of meditation whatever it is you want.

# A Glossary of Terms

Ballet poses are still called by their original French names. The reason for this is that ballet dancers have always felt that the essence of the movements are captured more fully in the original names. This is also true of the Sanskrit words used to describe many of the hatha asanas and the meditative practices. You will notice, if you attend a yoga class, and read other yoga books, that the name for some of the poses will vary. Perhaps this is because the practice of yoga is so much older than the first written collations of it. Nonetheless, many people find the original names, whether they are strictly correct or not, very soothing and excellent tools for tuning the mind into the activity.

**Abhaysa**
Sanskrit word for practice.

**Ahimsa**
The principle of nonviolence. One of the five abstinences outlined in Pantajali's *Yoga Sutras*.

**Ajna**
The sixth chakra, located between the eyebrows and referred to as the 'third eye'. It is the source of intellectual thought and insight.

## Agarigrapha
The principle of non-possessiveness. One of Pantajali's five abstinences.

## Asana
A hatha posture.

## Asteya
The principle of non-stealing, from Pantajali's five abstinences.

## Atman
The individual self.

## Bhakti yoga
One of the six paths of yoga, advocating devotion.

## Bhujangasana
The cobra asana.

## Brahman
The universal self.

## Bramachanya
The observance of continence.

## Chakra
A source of energy. There are seven, located along the body's central channel, the spine.

**Chakrasana**
The wheel asana, also known as 'the crab'.

**Dhanurasana**
The bow asana.

**Dharana**
The sixth limb of yoga, requiring the mind's learning to concentrate fully on an object.

**Dhyana**
The seventh limb of yoga, where the mind learns to contemplate.

**Gyana**
One of the six paths of yoga, advocating study.

**Gomukhasana**
The cow-face asana.

**Gunas**
The three different categories of foodstuffs according to yogic diet.

**Halasana**
The plough asana.

**Hatha yoga**
The only yoga discipline that involves physical movement.

**Ishvara prandihana**
Attentiveness to the Divine.

## Karma
One of the six paths of yoga, advocating actions.

## Kundalini
Literally means 'the coiled serpent'.

## Manipura
Chakra located in the solar plexus that is considered to be the source of the 'life force'.

## Mantra
A sound or chant repeated to aid meditation. Also the name given to one of the six paths of yoga, advocating the use of sound.

## Matyasana
The fish asana.

## Matsyendrasana
The spinal twist asana.

## Mayurasana
The peacock asana.

## Muladhara
The chakra located at the base of the spine, and said to be where the kundalini sleeps.

## Nadas
Mystic sounds used as an aid to meditation.

**Namis**
The channels which carry the 'life-force' throughout the body. Chakras are located where the namis intersect.

**Niyamanas**
The Sanskrit name for the observances outlined by Pantajali.

**Padmasana**
The lotus position.

**Prana**
The 'life force' or 'breath of life'.

**Pranayama**
The yogic system of breath control. Means literally 'interruption of breath'.

**Paschimotanasana**
The forward bend asana.

**Prasarita padottanasana**
The wide side-stretch asana.

**Pratyahara**
The fifth of the eight limbs of yoga, involving the mind's withdrawal from domination by the senses.

**Rajasic**
Food which is spicy and stimulating.

### Sahasraha
The chakra situated at the crown of the head and symbolised by the thousand-petalled lotus.

### Samadhi
The eighth limb of yoga, when superconsciousness is achieved.

### Samprayana
Awareness of all things.

### Santosha
The principle of contentment. One of Pantajali's five observances.

### Satu bhandasana
The bridge asana.

### Sattva
Harmony.

### Sattvic
Pure foods.

### Sarvangasana
The shoulder stand asana.

### Satya
The principle of truthfulness and integrity. One of Pantajali's five abstinences.

**Saucha**
The observance of purity.

**Shavasana**
The corpse asana, for relaxation.

**Siddhis**
The psychic powers that ancient yogis claimed came about through meditative practice.

**Simhasana**
The lion asana.

**Sitali**
The cooling breath.

**Surya namaskar**
The 'salute to the sun'.

**Sushumna**
The central channel of the body, corresponding with the spine.

**Tadasana**
The mountain asana.

**Tamasic**
Foods which are fermented or overripe.

**Tapas**
The principle of austerity. One of Pantajali's five observances.

**Trikonasana**
The triangle asana.

**Vairagya**
Non-attachment.

**Vajrasana**
The thunderbolt asana.

**Vishuddha**
The chakra located at the branchial plexus, said to induce fruitful study.

**Vrittis**
Thought waves.

**Vrksasana**
The tree asana.

**Yoga**
The harnessing of mental and physical energy, the mind to the body, to achieve a higher consciousness.

**Yogi**
An expert in the art of yoga.